D1580565

Battleground Europe
MAMETZ WOOD

Battleground series:

Battleground Europe

MAMETZ WOOD

MICHAEL RENSHAW

First World War Series Editor
Nigel Cave

Pen & Sword
MILITARY

First published in Great Britain in 1999 by Leo Cooper

Reprinted in 2006 and 2011 by
PEN & SWORD MILITARY
An imprint of
Pen & Sword Books Ltd
47 Church Street
Barnsley
South Yorkshire
S70 2AS

Copyright © Michael Renshaw 1999, 2006, 2011

ISBN 978 0 85052 664 6

The right of Michael Renshaw to be identified as Author of this work has been asserted
by him in accordance with the Copyright, Designs and Patents Act 1988.

A CIP catalogue record for this book is
available from the British Library

All rights reserved. No part of this book may be reproduced or transmitted in
any form or by any means, electronic or mechanical including photocopying,
recording or by any information storage and retrieval system, without
permission from the Publisher in writing.

Printed and bound by
CPI Group (UK) Ltd, Croydon, CR0 4YY

Pen & Sword Books Ltd incorporates the Imprints of Pen & Sword Aviation,
Pen & Sword Family History, Pen & Sword Maritime, Pen & Sword Military,
Pen & Sword Discovery, Wharncliffe Local History, Wharncliffe True Crime,
Wharncliffe Transport, Pen & Sword Select, Pen & Sword Military Classics,
Leo Cooper, The Praetorian Press, Remember When,
Seaforth Publishing and Frontline Publishing

For a complete list of Pen & Sword titles please contact
PEN & SWORD BOOKS LIMITED
47 Church Street, Barnsley, South Yorkshire, S70 2AS, England
E-mail: enquiries@pen-and-sword.co.uk
Website: www.pen-and-sword.co.uk

CONTENTS

INTRODUCTION BY SERIES EDITOR

Mametz Wood is the largest of the woods over which the British and German armies fought in the long, desperate struggle of the summer and autumn of 1916. Its great expanse covers much of the ground between the German First (based on Mametz and Fricourt) and Second lines (based on Bazentin le Petit). Of the woods that were fought over at the Somme it might not have been the most hard fought over (that dubious distinction falls to High Wood) nor the most popularly known to the contemporary traveller (Delville Wood takes that place) but the hard fought battle of the early days of July 1916 has caught the popular imagination and nowhere more so than in Wales.

Mametz Wood does not appear in the battlefield nomenclature report compiled after the war. The fighting that took place, chiefly between the 5th – 9th July, but carrying on until the 11th, is officially incorporated within the Battle of Albert. It is not even a 'Tactical Incident'.

Yet the fighting that took place here was of great importance for the development of the Battle of the Somme, that great struggle that lasted for well over four and a half months. It was considered vital that this wood should be removed as an obstacle before the next stage of the battle could proceed. It was to cost much in blood and reputations. Men of great literary renown fought through here, amongst them Frank Richards, Siegfried Sassoon and Robert Graves.

This area of the Somme has always been of personal significance to me. It was just to the east of the wood that my grandfather's battalion, 7/Leicesters, lay out on the ground prior to the dawn assault on Bazentin le Petit Wood on 14th July 1916. His diary tersely records the sad events of that and subsequent days and the traumatic calling of the roll when the battalion came out of the line in the nearby remnants of Fricourt Wood.

In recent years the heroic endeavours of the Welsh Division, 'Lloyd George's Welsh Army', have been fittingly commemorated, above all by the placing in 1987 of the Dragon Memorial on its prominent position overlooking the wood. This was the result of the dedicated work of a number of people, particularly in the South Wales branch of the Western Front Association, and of the generosity of the local landowner. Numerous people now make their way along a typical Somme track and sit and contemplate the scene, now in peaceful tranquillity.

Mametz Wood has been well served by its most recent historian, Colin Hughes. His book, *Mametz – Lloyd George's 'Welsh Army' on the Somme*, first published in 1982, and one of the first books of its type, is a great tribute to the men who fought here. Michael Renshaw has continued that tribute by also telling the story of the 17th Northern Division who attempted to break through the western defences of the Wood and thereby the complete story of the Battle is now told.

Finally, a plea. In a sense it is probably wasted on the readers of this book, who will be far too sensible to engage in the sort of activities that bring, by association, all visitors to the woods and fields of the Somme a bad name. But still, I shall say it all the same. Please respect the land and the people who work it. We walk these fields and woods with their consent; act responsibly, seek permission, do not go about digging, do not block agricultural tracks. Instead, look and wonder at the sacrifice another generation made.

Nigel Cave
Ely Place, London

Be on your guard! The debris of war.

THE SOMME BATTLEFIELDS TODAY

A Frenchman employed by the Commonwealth War Graves Commission for over twenty years recently asked me why there had been such an increase in the number of visitors to the cemeteries in recent years. He explained to me that when he first started working for the Commission he might notice one coach a week touring the Somme battlefields, and if someone came to visit a grave the maintenance crew would normally stop work and stand aside whilst the pilgrimage was completed. Now, it is not unusual to see five or six coaches a day and if work stopped when a visit was made to a cemetery very little would get done in a day!

Since the days of the Battle of Crecy when the Earl of Northampton and Edward III's son aged 16 – The Black Prince, The Prince of Wales, defeated the French, war has come to the Somme. When the Black Prince sent a message for reinforcements to his father who was watching the battle in reserve from the rear the reply was 'let him win his spurs'.

So it was intended for Kitchener's Army to 'win their spurs' on the Somme, but as we know the outcome was to be rather different.

The battlefields are found in the northern part of this Départment which takes its name from the river which flows through the region. Flow is, perhaps, not quite the correct description as the 'river' is most unusual in that it consists of a continuous series of lakes, lagoons and inlets all carefully worked by a network of sluices to control the water levels. There is a man-made navigation canal and on it both large and small boats ply what seems to be a lucra. /e trade. All this flows to the sea via the Bay of the Somme.

The river Ancre is a tributary of the Somme and flows down the valley through the northern part of the battlefield from Miraumont through Beaumont, Hamel, Aveluy and on to Albert finally joining the Somme near the pleasant town of Corbie with its fine abbey. The valley is very heavily wooded with lovely meadows and lakes adjoining its banks and is rich in fish so attracting many fishermen to its quiet waters.

Elsewhere, especially east of the Albert Bapaume road the countryside is open and rolling. Sadly many trees and hedgerows have disappeared but large tracts of woodland still exist today that existed before and during the war.

Many thought nature could never recover and that no-one could farm and live there again but for the most part life here on the Somme

Winter time in the wood – then and now.

through the effort of man and nature has returned to normal so that to the uninitiated it is hard to realise that anything on the scale of the First World War happened here. Of course the cemeteries and memorials give the lie to that impression and the sight of the local farmers' stockpile of unexploded shells awaiting collection are another reminder.

Deep dugouts and trenches were often filled in with the broken brick and general rubble of the shattered villages so it is not uncommon to see traces of red brick and slate across the middle of a field when it is ploughed or similar material falling away from the banks of 'sunken roads'.

In the same way the villages were rebuilt where previous occupants lived. The villages in this part of Picardie are traditionally the familiar design that provides large barns fronting the roadside while in the rear the farmhouse is connected in a rectangle by accommodation for the animals at each side. Thereby people and animals live closely together. It is the exception to find a farm standing alone in the middle of the fields such as we are more used to in Britain.

I remember showing the *Beaumont Hamel* book in this series of Battlefield Europe to a resident of the village. He was very keen to see it but on opening it his mood changed 'It's in English, I can't read it', he said, clearly disappointed.

On another occasion a young woman from Beaumont Hamel who lives and works in Manchester told us of a visit she made to Edinburgh Castle, where she was amazed to see the name of her village on the memorial, 'I never knew my village was so famous' she told me.

This then is the briefest glimpse of the countryside of the Somme. 'Where is everybody?' visitors often ask. It is very quiet there is a sense of space and tranquillity strangely it seems, of almost inverse proportions to the violence of its past.

Many remark on its atmosphere without being able to explain it. Others come to visit and leave feeling compelled to return. As one visitor said to me 'Once you have been to the Somme it touches you in a way that you can never let go'.

I have dedicated this book to my late father-in-law, Harold Llewellyn, born in Cwmbach, who after the premature loss of my own father became much a second father to me, but who was also lost to his own family prematurely.

Auchonvillers, Somme 1998

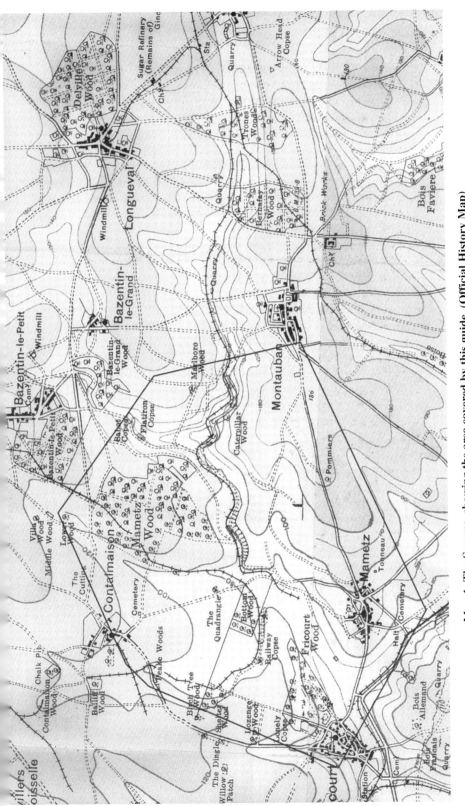

Map 1. The Somme, showing the area covered by this guide. (Official History Map)

ACKNOWLEDGEMENTS

Throughout the preparation of this book many people have contributed in some way on its journey to final completion.

I would especially like to thank Huw Rodge for his support from the outset. Sean Joyce gave his considerable expertise in preparing the maps. Trevor Tasker provided many examples of his collection of photographs and ephemera. David Petersen gave details of the design and construction of the Red Dragon Memorial. Peter Rolland of The Commonwealth War Graves Commission at Beaurains, France.

I thank staff at The Public Record Office, The Imperial War Museum, The Royal Welsh Fusiliers Museum at Caernarvon and The Museum of Rugby at Twickenham.

I acknowledge permission given by Mr George Sassoon to use abridged extracts from *Memoirs of an Infantry Officer*. To Faber and Faber for permission to reproduce extracts from *In Parenthesis* by David Jones. Brian Stokes, King's College, Wimbledon for supplying a picture of Lionel Duncan Stanbury. Terry Rogers, Marlborough College; Rusty MacLean, Rugby School; M. K. Swales, Denstone College.

In addition I would like to thank the following: Edward and Elizabeth Dunston John Angus Evans, Julie Renshaw, Joan Lovatt, Michael Fellows, Mr Len Mullins of *The Western Telegraph*, Sandra Poulton, Frances Speakman, Glenys Williams, John and June Williams.

Lastly and most importantly, I pay tribute to the men who did it all. No words here can adequately reflect what they went through and what they were prepared to sacrifice.

Their diaries, letters and other records are reproduced by permission of The Public Record Office.

A collapsed trench mortar position - Beaumont Hamel.

Chapter One

PROLOGUE
1/2 July

On 1 July 1916 the British Army launched a major offensive on German positions established on the chalk uplands of the Départment of the Somme. These positions were linked around seven villages which had been turned into veritable fortresses from Serre in the north to Maricourt in the south.

Neither the place nor the time was of British choosing. The Commander-in-Chief General Sir Douglas Haig would have preferred ground further to the north and had argued that the recently recruited 'New' Volunteer Army was not ready for such an operation. However the French were under intense pressure at Verdun. That battle which commenced in February 1916 which has been called the 'graveyard of the French nation' was 'bleeding' France to death. The French argued that the British must do something to help relieve the pressure on Verdun and draw some of the German fire power.

In the days before the battle an artillery barrage without precedent covered the German lines, the guns stood almost wheel to wheel for

Trench mortar position during the Somme battle.   TAYLOR LIBRARY

British 6 inch howitzers moving to positions along the Albert-Fricourt road during the battle. It is estimated that half a million shells failed to explode and that the German wire had not been cut sufficiently for the British to get into the German trenches. TAYLOR LIBRARY

sixteen miles. One and a half million shells poured out and it is said the noise of the barrage could be heard in London. At 7.30am on 1 July the British, confident of success moved across No Man's Land only to be caught in a hail of machine-gun and rifle fire. The Germans had dug deeply into the chalk and constructed huge shelters, from which they emerged relatively untouched by the barrage. In addition through faulty manufacture by unskilled labour or lack of training by the gunners, it is estimated that half a million of the shells did not explode and that the German wire had not been cut sufficiently for the British to get into the German trenches.

1 July 1916 was the greatest disaster ever suffered by the British Army: 19,240 were killed and 35,493 wounded and into these shattered remains the 38th Welsh Division came marching from St Pol to the battle for Mametz Wood. Although Mametz Wood will be forever associated with the 38th Welsh Division it was not entirely a Welsh affair and it is important to understand the action in the days leading up to their involvement in the capture of the wood. The original intention was to attack the wood from the south-west and this task was to be undertaken largely by the 7th Division who would be supported on their left by the 17th Division.

17th (Northern)

The 17th Division came into the line at Fricourt

14

relieving its own 50 Brigade which had already been in action attached to the 21st Division. All these divisions were part of the British Fourth Army, XV Corps with headquarters at Heilly which was commanded by Lieutenant-General H S Horne.

At 9.00am on the evening of 1 July, Brigadier-General R B Fell commanding 51 Brigade was summoned to the 17th Division Headquarters and rode over to Meaulte on his horse. There he met Major-General T D Pilcher commanding officer of the 17th Division who told him he was intending to withdraw 50 Brigade after the losses they had suffered that day and replace them with 51 Brigade. However it was also his intention to put Brigadier-General W J T Glasgow commanding the ill-fated 50 Brigade in charge of Fell's 51 Brigade as he had already seen the ground.

Major-General Pilcher, however, was not prepared for the state in

View of the ground over which 8th South Staffordshire's and 7th Lincolnshire's attacked Fricourt.

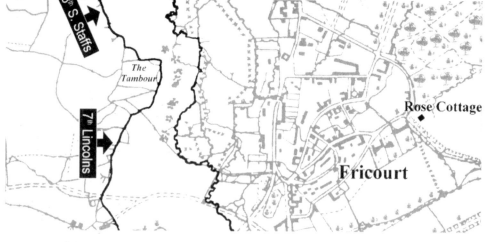

Map 2. The capture of Fricourt 2 July 1916.

which he found Brigadier-General Glasgow who was quite 'broken
down' over the losses he had witnessed among his men that day and
after talks lasting into the early hours of 2 July it was finally agreed
that Brigadier-General Fell should remain in command.

After the disastrous scenes of the first day the night of 1/2 July was
relatively quiet. During the night the Germans began to withdraw from
the village to a new defensive position called Railway Alley which
linked on the left to Lozenge Trench. Patrols of the 7th Division
entered Fricourt unopposed in the early hours of 2 July and together
with patrols the 8th South Staffordshire Regiment (17th Division)
captured about one hundred men of the German 11th Reserve
Regiment. It was the information obtained from these prisoners about
German movements that persuaded Major-General Pilcher to order an
immediate attack. Patrols of the 8th South Staffordshires gallantly led
by Lieutenant Turney made good progress flushing out pockets of
Germans and were reported to be in Lozenge Trench by noon, but
reported that the 7th Lincolns had not occupied Railway Alley which
was an extension to the right of the trench they held. The 7th Lincolns
Battalion diary records they did not move forward until 12.15pm (the
original time of the attack). Battle patrols, led by Lieutenant Kimber
and Lieutenant Barrett advanced, supported by four companies.
Having taken some prisoners they were held up at 2.10pm at Rose
Cottage. The Germans still had machine guns positioned in Fricourt
Wood and it was over 3 hours later at 5.20 pm before the 7th Lincolns
were able to report its capture during which they lost one officer killed
in action, Captain Dickinson, and 19 other ranks wounded.

Later that night as darkness fell bombers of the 10th Sherwood
Foresters attacked Railway Alley which was well wired and strongly

7 Lincoln Regt
25/6/1916

My Dear Mother and Tess

In a very great hurry I pen these few lines to you and hope that they will find you A1. I am enclosing a cheque for two pounds which I am sending rather earlier than usual in as much as I may not be able to write or send to you for a few days. We are going to do probably a little hard work and in the course of the next few days I must beg of you to remember me in all your prayers and pray for our safe journey and success and ask all friends the same favour. If you can afford a mass or two for me I can assure you I can do with all the benefits reaped from them. Don't let this letter worry you too much and the only help you can give me is not to worry but to pray for my safety. I am going to do my duty so you mustn't worry. Write to me as usual and I shall let you know as soon as I can how I am getting on. I went to Holy Communion and I am fairly well prepared. I am feeling perfectly fit and only hoping all will be well.

Remember me in your prayers and look on the bright side of things and hope for my safe return. I will write to you as soon as I can I only hope that this letter won't upset you. I thought I should let you know in case I shouldn't be able to write for a short time. Give my very best love to all and remember me to all old friends. Now don't worry because I shall write as soon as I can. I have arranged for all my money and things should anything happen and everything goes to you. I think this is all so will conclude with heaps of love. Your affectionate son Cyril.

Remember always I am only doing my duty and this should make you feel more settled. If God spares me all will be well. Goodbye 'til I write again. Cyril

Last letter written by Lieutenant Barrett prior to the attack on Fricourt village 2 July 1916. The fears of a man about to attack the German lines comes through in this communication home.

Fricourt after it had been captured by 17th Division. TAYLOR LIBRARY

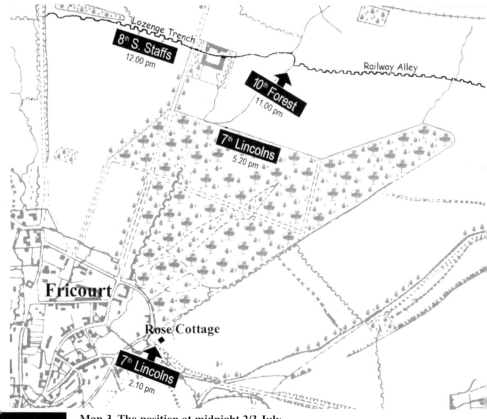

Map 3. The position at midnight 2/3 July.

held and entering it from the left hand end fought up a distance of 200 yards of the trench.

That morning the 7th Division had been ordered to patrol forward at 7.30am north of Mametz village. Enemy movement was seen in Bottom Wood and the 2nd Queens assisted by the 1st South Staffordshires took a heavy toll of retreating Germans. Of about 200 all were killed or wounded with the exception of about ten who got away. By 11.00am the 2nd Queens were in Cliff Trench and by 2.00pm in White Trench. A machine gun and several prisoners were taken and later two 77mm field guns were also found nearby. Work immediately commenced on digging in. The trenches, especially White Trench was only partly dug and while work progressed the German shelling continued. The 21st Manchesters came up in support and at 10.30pm repulsed a small counter attack.

Thus at nightfall on 2/3 July the objectives set for the first day had been achieved and on the right British troops of the 7th Division on Fusilier Ridge overlooked the southern end of Mametz Wood.

Chapter Two

THE CAPTURE OF RAILWAY ALLEY
3 July

At 9.00am the attack was renewed. The 7th Borders immediately came under machine gun fire as they advanced from the front of Fricourt Wood towards Railway Alley. The officers leading the battle patrols were Captain Crosse and Second-Lieutenant Crompton who always carried a Lewis gun when going into the attack but both officers soon became casualties. The 7th Borders were supported by the 7th Lincolns who twice that morning at 10.50am and 11.40am were called in to send reinforcements of battalion bombers and Lewis gun crews. Similarly drawn into the attack were detachments of the 8th South Staffordshires and 10th Sherwood Foresters.

It was not until 11.30am that Railway Alley was entered and finally cleared by 1.20pm.

During the night of 2nd/3rd patrols of the 21st Manchesters (7th Division) had been pushed forward into Bottom Wood and had remained there before the advance of the 7th Borders, and were under heavy machine gun fire. An interesting account exists of the events given by Colonel W Norman of the 21st Manchesters who states that:

> *'About 1.55am a message was received that the 17th Division was to attack on the line Shelter Wood, Birch Tree Wood and Bottom Wood, at 9 am.*
>
> *About 8.30 am I moved up to the advanced company HQ and learnt that a patrol had during the night entered Bottom Wood and found it apparently clear. I sent two strong patrols into the wood under Lieutenants Thorniley and Farnsworth. As they*

Railway Alley ran diagonally from the right hand end of the wood to bottom left. The 7th Borders attacked from the right.

entered the wood, under my observation, a small party of Germans bolted in front of them. These were evidently artillerymen for they emerged from behind a low bluff where we found three guns. As these men bolted one of our shells dropped among them and they scattered in a north-easterly direction. It was nearly time for the contemplated attack, and, I came to the conclusion that the shot was the precursor of a barrage in front of the attack. I at once sent to recall the patrols. Lieutenant Farnsworth returned, but, Lieutenant Thorniley had gone too far. He eventually reached the point where Bottom Alley emerged from Bottom Wood, and held that point, after reporting to me that all was clear. Soon after our attack was seen coming through the edge of Fricourt Wood, but there were no signs of any advance on its left along Willow Avenue. It appeared that there must be a wide gap between their right and my left, I accordingly sent a company to occupy the wood and to make connection. Considerably later a company (7/Border) appeared coming up Willow Avenue, and entered Bottom Wood but seeing it held by my men inclined to its left.'

By 3.00pm the line held ran from the front of Bottom Wood along the long hedge towards towards Shelter Wood.

An advance was also made on the left in the 21st Division sector

Map 4. The capture of Railway Alley and Bottom Wood.

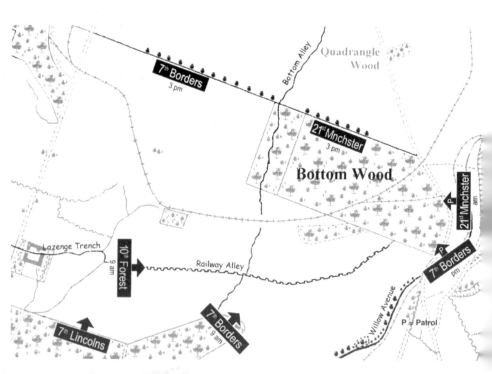

Site of Crucifix Trench with Shelter Wood behind.

and Crucifix Trench and Shelter Wood captured, including a whole battalion of the 186th Regiment with its Commanding Officer. One German officer hid a grenade in his hat and suddenly threw it at an unsuspecting British soldier killing him instantly. The officer was immediately taken away separately to be tried by a court martial.

The surrender of the German battalion had left a gap in their line and Colonel Norman continues:

'I had gone over to interview the O.C. 7/Borders. On my return I found my men walking about most unconcernedly in the open, outside the wood and in full view and easy range of Quadrangle Trench. A patrol had entered the copse called Quadrangle Wood and reported that it contained a couple of dummy guns.

Though within easy range of Quadrangle Trench not a shot was fired at us from that trench or from Mametz Wood.'

Brigadier General Fell wrote later of the events of 3 July:

'I then received orders from the division to take Railway Alley, Railway Copse, Crucifix Trench and Bottom Wood, and then consolidate in front of Quadrangle Trench. This we did with a loss of about 600 men and we captured the Commanding Officer and what remained of the 186th Regiment of Germans, who surrendered to us, we also got some of the 13th, 111th and 118th Regiments, and also 3 guns, machine guns and a huge underground dug-out full of food and stores. On the morning of the 3rd I was down at Fricourt seeing the Borders go on, slapping them on their backs being countrymen of mine, when General Pilcher arrived he was very angry, said he had been to Brigade HQ and could not find me there and gave me a direct verbal order not again to leave my brigade HQ without his permission. In the evening he came again and I told him we had the Germans stone cold in Quadrangle Trench and I was satisfied we could take it there and then. General Pilcher however disagreed.'

Meanwhile on the right the 7th Division consolidated. The 1st South

German prisoners taken in the opening stages of the Battle of the Somme.
TAYLOR LIBRARY

Staffordshires took up position in Bottom Wood and linked with the 8th South Staffordshires of the 17th Division, and many greetings from old friends were exchanged. The excavations in Cliff Trench and White Trench were completed and the 2nd Queens were still in position overlooking the southern part of Mametz Wood and Bottom Wood.

As the patrols of the 21st Manchesters sent in by Colonel Norman at 8.30am reached Bottom Wood so parties of Germans were driven into the open and bolted towards the comparative safety of Quadrangle Wood and the trench beyond it. At a range of about 1,000 yards the Lewis gunners of the 2nd Queens dug in on Fusilier Ridge had them easily in their sights and many of the Germans became casualties.

Patrols sent out during the afternoon at 2.00pm had found Mametz Wood and Quadrangle Trench empty but no orders were issued until 8.15pm from XV Corps. These directed the 7th Division to occupy the southern end of Mametz Wood along Strip Trench and Wood Trench to Quadrangle Trench. This would assist the 17th Division which was to approach Mametz Wood from the west.

Night of 3/4 July The First Attack on Mametz Wood

Two battalions, the 1st Royal Welsh Fusiliers and the 2nd Royal Irish were detailed to carry out the attack of the 7th Division.

Soon after midnight on 3/4 July the two battalions left the railway halt at Mametz. The guides of the 1st Royal Welsh Fusiliers lost their way with the result that the Fusiliers did not reach the deploying position until about 6.00am when it was already getting light and too late to attack.

Second Lieutenant Siegfried Sassoon who was serving with the 1st Royal Welsh Fusiliers later wrote a brief account of the wasted journey made by the Fusiliers.

Original XV Corps map showing the battle area for Mametz Wood covered by this book.

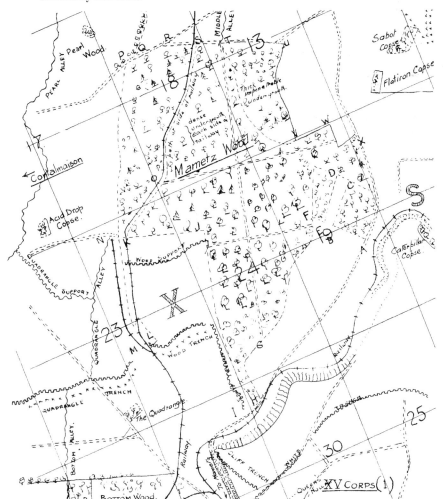

'*July 4   4.30am*

The Battalion started at 9.15pm yesterday and, after messing about for over four hours, got going with tools, wire, etc. and went through Mametz, up a long communication-trench. Came down across the open hillside looking across to Mametz Wood, and out at the end of Bright Alley. Found that the Royal Irish were being bombed and machine-gunned by Bosches in the wood, and had fifteen wounded. A still grey morning; red east; everyone very tired.'

The 2nd Royal Irish attacked under the impression that Quadrangle Trench was in British possession. The narrative of the 2nd Royal Irish War Diary describes what happened:

'In the evening about 7.30pm the Battalion received orders to march via Mametz and consolidate the line Quadrangle Trench - Wood Trench - Strip Trench and to make a reconnaissance of Mametz Wood. The three trenches were stated to be in our hands and it was also mentioned that probably no resistance would be encountered in Mametz Wood. The Battalion was heavily encumbered with materials for consolidating and was halted on the road first south of Strip Trench for a rest. Lieutenant Tod and the Battalion scouts were sent out to reconnoitre Strip Trench and one of the scouts returned almost immediately with a prisoner who informed us that there were a considerable number of Germans in the wood. As the CO understood that the 1/R Welsh Fusiliers were in position on our right he ordered an immediate attack on the Mametz Wood before the approach of

Railway halt at Mametz 1998.

Road where the 2nd Royal Irish halted before entering the wood to the left.

daylight would reveal to the enemy that a battalion was halted in fours along a road within 100 yards of their position, so the Grenade coy was ordered to attack Strip Trench with D coy in support, while A and C coys formed a defensive flank facing towards Quadrangle and Wood Trenches both of which contrary to our information were discovered to be very strongly held by Germans. The Grenade coy almost immediately got touch with the enemy and succeeded in bombing along Strip Trench almost as far as its junction with Wood Trench. The enemy was at this point strongly reinforced from the wood which was very dense and impenetrable and the Grenade coys were gradually bombed back again and forced to fall back on their Supports which were also heavily engaged with the enemy. Enemy machine gun fire of great intensity was coming from the east of Mametz Wood and a heavy cross-fire from Quadrangle Trench which made our whole position untenable. The CO ordered a retirement to be made to a position about 300 yards back which afforded some cover, and applied for artillery support so that he could effect a retirement to

The remains of Strip Trench (note the unexploded shells).

25

Mametz. This retirement was eventually accomplished and the Battalion mustered again at Mansel Copse. The retirement was made reluctantly as many casualties had been inflicted on the enemy and on one occasion a footing had been effected in the wood and two field guns captured. But the failure of the 1/R Welsh Fusiliers to get into position on our right and the strength of the enemy who was being rapidly reinforced made it imperative to retire. Our casualties were 75 all ranks. Lieutenant Usher and 2/Lt Kerr were killed leading attacks on Strip Trench. The former had been wounded but refused to leave his platoon. 2/Lt Perrin was wounded by a bomb in the leg which killed the German who threw it - this officer killed two Germans with bombs after being wounded. CSU Hayes was wounded in a gallant attempt to save Lieutenant Usher's life. Attached is a copy of narrative by Captain Colter who commanded D Coy.'

The position of the 2nd Royal Irish was impossible and they had no alternative to withdraw. They brought back the breech blocks of two guns found near the bank between Bottom Wood and Mametz Wood.

At XV Corps a somewhat more optimistic view of the night's events was taken. Although in possession of a patrol report, all the problems encountered seem to have been overlooked in favour of information taken from the prisoner who said that he was a member of only one patrol in the wood and that everyone else had retreated. This information differed from that which the same prisoner gave to the 2nd Royal Irish.

The report in their possession was written by Captain Colter of D Company and it is an interesting record of the unsuccessful attack on Strip Trench. It shows an appreciation of what was going on about him while he was leading his own company. Considering the attack took place in darkness, it is remarkable how he was able to produce a map of the area attacked (immediately recognisable today) and the position of enfilading machine gun fire.

On 4 July Siegfried Sassoon recorded

'This morning the facts were: R.W.F. and Royal Irish were sent up to consolidate trenches close to the south-east end of Mametz Wood and to clear the wood outskirts. The Irish got there and found enemy machine-guns and bombers and snipers in the wood, which is of big old trees. Our A Company went forward to join them but were sniped on the road and got into a quarry where they lost four wounded and one killed. The Irish

On the Evening of the 4th July 1916
The Regiment received orders to ~~march~~
out ~~~~ and consolidate the line
Quadrangle Trench, Wood Trench and
Strip Trench and reconnoitre part of
Mametz wood. We were ~~~~ certainly
led to expect no opposition from the
enemy. We arrived at our outposts about
2 a.m in the morning of 5th July. Lt Tod.
and the battalion scouts pushed ahead to
Mametz wood and entered strip Trench.
One prisoner was taken who had lost his way
~~while~~ ~~out~~ returning with hot coffee to his
patrol. He said his patrol numbered
about 40 men and it was the outpost of
the Regiment stationed in the Grosse Wald
i.e Mametz wood or Bazentin le Grand
wood.

We understood that The Welsh Fusiliers would
be on our right entrenching along Fusilier Ridge
they were however led wrongly by their guide
and did not arrive. Also we were given to
understand that Quadrangle Trench was

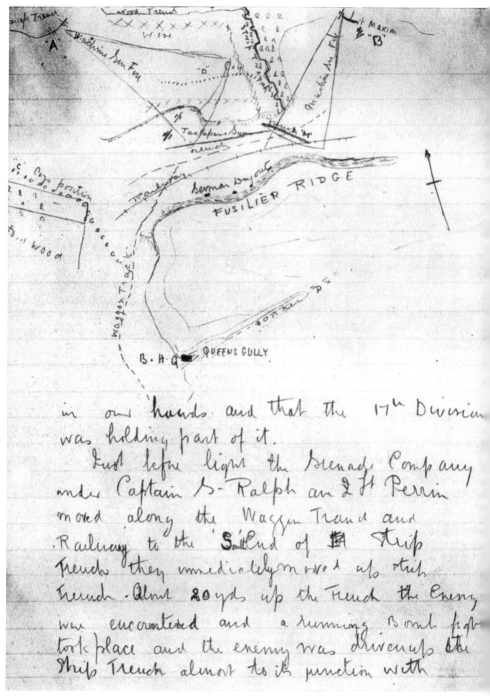

in our hands. and that the 17th Division
was holding part of it.

Just before light the Grenade Company
under Captain S. Ralph an 2 Lt Perrin
moved along the Waggon Trand and
Railway to the 'S'End of Strip
Trench they immediately moved up strip
Trench. About 20 yds up the Trench the Enemy
were encountered and a running Bomb fight
took place and the enemy was drivenup the
Ship Trench almost to its junction with

28

"Wood Trench. During this time "D"
Company moved over the open to on the
left of the Grenade Company in order to
get Flank fire to bear on the enemy +
so to obtain possession of Wood and
Strip Trench. When about ½ way across
the open heavy machine gun fire was
opened on "D" Company from point "A" in
Quadrangle Trench and several casualties
occurred in order to get out of the fire zone
that part of "D" Company between the German
Wire + Strip Trench got into Strip Trench
while the remainder outside the Wire were order
to retire and hold the bank (where two $
German Guns had also been discovered
hurriedly left by the Enemy). The enemy had
meanwhile been strongly reinforced and the
Bombing fight was continued but our bombs
began to give out and we retired slowly down
Strip trench and held the outskirts of Wood,
Trench "M", and bank just North of German
Guns. here we held out and the enemy were
unable to advance further

The Position was naturally strong and reinforcement by "A" & "B" Companies made us perfectly safe in our new position.

The fight continued unceasingly but both sides being in good positions neither side was able to make any further advance. And the Brigadier ordered our retirement.

Our Casualties practically confined to the Grenade & "D" Company were heavy but those of the enemy were at least equal if not more. and the knowledge that the Enemy ~~was~~ intended to hold Mametz wood was of great value to the G.O.C.

Lt Usher & 2/Lt Kerr of "D" Company were killed and 21 other ranks were Killed and wounded

2/Lt Perin of the Grenade Company was wounded & close on 50 other ranks were killed and wounded

There were 3 or 4 other casualties in the remainder of the Battalion. The 2nd Engagement taking about 12 hours later in precisely the same place is not covered by these casualties.

Showing the bank where the 2nd Royal Irish found two German guns. Mametz Wood (Strip Trench in background).

meanwhile had tried to bomb the Bosches in the wood, failed entirely and suffered 60 casualties (one officer killed and one wounded). Our guns then chucked a lot of heavy shrapnel over the wood and the Irish got away. The whole thing seems to have been caused by bad staff work (of the Division). We were out eleven hours and got back to our field about 8.30am.'

The guns from which the Royal Irish took the breech blocks.

While all this was going on the Germans were actively re-occupying Quadrangle Trench and re-inforcing Mametz Wood and what might have been a simple task several hours previously was now going to be a much larger and more costly operation. The absence of orders for a more substantial attack may be due to Lieutenant-General Horne's presence at a Corps Commanders' Conference during the afternoon of 3 July. There was disagreement on General Rawlinson's plans to attack the German second line at Bazentin. General Haig would not agree to the assault before both Mametz Wood and Trones Wood had been captured and any threat of counter attacks on both flanks thereby avoided.

The Official Historian concluded:

'It would appear that if XV Corps had encouraged more vigorous action on the afternoon of the 3rd, a hold on Mametz Wood could have been secured and Wood Trench and Quadrangle Trench occupied.'

Chapter Three

THE DEFENDERS OF QUADRANGLE TRENCH
ARE SURPRISED
4 July

In the absence of any orders troops were engaged during the early part of the day in clearing the battlefield of the previous three days. In the 17th Division Sector while the wounded had been attended to, no attempt had been made to clear the battlefield of the dead. Brigadier-General J L J Clarke in command of 52 Brigade recalled:

'In the old no man's land the bodies of our men were to be seen just as they fell in every conceivable attitude, some prone, others huddled up in a crouching position, or kneeling in the act of firing, all stark and rigid like so many wax work figures; in the captured German trenches the dead in places were literally piled up in heaps friend and foe mixed up in an extricable mess where hand to hand fighting had taken place.'

It will be recalled that the previous day Brigadier General Fell had been in trouble with General Pilcher for being absent from Brigade Headquarters in Fricourt Chateau. On the 4th at 2.00pm Pilcher came from Meaulte to Fricourt again to see Fell and this time found Fell at

Soldiers of both sides witnessed such scenes as they advanced over captured ground. Here, five Germans lie in a captured trench.

'Heavy rain fell all afternoon with thunderstorms and the trenches soon filled up with water and everything turned to mud. The troops were soaked through and completely clogged up.' TAYLOR LIBRARY

his post still very frustrated and anxious to make an attack. Pilcher told him it might be possible for his brigade to make an attack on the Quadrangle at midnight. Fell recalled, 'I told him again, we hold the Bosche stone cold and I had scouts up trees watching them going and coming'.

By 5.15pm orders were issued that Fell's brigade were to be relieved by 52 Brigade. A disappointed Fell was spoken to by Pilcher who told him he was proud of what his men had done and he wanted 52 Brigade to do likewise. Fell's disappointment at being withdrawn before the attack was shared with some of his troops. The 10th Sherwood Foresters waiting in Hedge Line Trench were reported as "being anxious to capture that trench" (Quadrangle). So Fell's 51 Brigade gave way to 52 Brigade and the 10th Sherwood Foresters were replaced by the 9th Northumberland Fusiliers. The 7th Lincolns and the 7th Borders also gave way but relief for the 8th South Staffordshires was short lived as they rejoined the front line attached temporarily to the newly arrived 52 Brigade.

Heavy rain fell all afternoon with thunderstorms and the trenches soon filled up with water and everything turned to mud. The troops were soaked through and completely clogged up.

The battle plan was to stage a surprise attack at midnight on 4/5 July on Quadrangle Trench and Wood Trench but Major-General H E Watts commanding the 7th Division telephoned XV Corps Headquarters at 6.15pm to say that it was impossible to make a surprise attack because of the conditions. Lieutenant General Horne was unwilling to cancel the attack but changed the orders to include a preliminary bombardment. The attack was retimed to start at 12.45am.

During the afternoon a bombardment was launched to cut the German wire and final reports were that the wire in front of Quadrangle Trench was well gapped but there was only one gap in the centre of Wood Trench. The night was very dark and the ground very heavy and conditions quite appalling as another bombardment started at 12.15am on 5 July prior to the attack timed for 12.45am.

5 July

The assault was to be made on a front of about 1,800 yards. There were four assaulting battalions. On the extreme left flank were the 10th Lancashire Fusiliers, on their right the 9th Northumberland Fusiliers and the 1st Royal Welsh Fusiliers were in the centre with the 2nd Royal Irish on the right flank.

During the bombardment the fighting patrols crept out into the darkness of No Man's Land to get as near to the German position as

Map 5. Attack on Quadrangle Trench and Wood Trench 5 July.

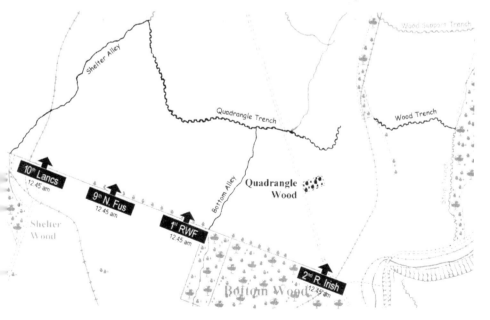

View of Hedgeline and Bottom Wood from the 10th Lancashire Fusilier's position. 9th Northumberland Fusiliers were in the middle distance and 1st Royal Welsh Fusiliers near Bottom Wood. (See Map 5)

possible. The barrage lifted and was replaced with a hail of machine gun fire. On the 7th Division front alone eight gun crews of 22 Brigade Machine Gun Company poured 6,500 rounds on to the front of Wood Trench and the eastern part of Quadrangle Trench. The assaulting troops charged in as swiftly as the conditions would allow and the enemy were taken by surprise, as had been originally intended.

On the extreme left of the attack the 10th Lancashire Fusiliers encountered some resistance. The Fusiliers were met by machine gun and rifle fire and a hotly contested fight took place before the trench was captured. Captain Thacker then led a patrol up from Quadrangle Trench up Pearl Alley nearly as far as Contalmaison and established a 'stop' in the trench, although this was later driven in by the Germans. Later the Fusiliers captured Shelter Alley and thus formed a defensive flank facing north-west. The 9th Northumberland Fusiliers rushed to the trench and met no severe rifle or machine gunfire. Major Allen gallantly led the attack setting a fine example, always in the forefront of the advance. 'A' Company especially, responded, doing good work, but in the process lost their commander Lieutenant Drummond. Many of the Germans were already dead in the trench killed by the artillery bombardment. Those that remained were bayoneted while those that retreated were pursued by Lewis gunners and rifle fire. Two enemy machine guns were captured and a large number of documents were sent back to Brigade Headquarters. By 1.30am the trench had been consolidated and four machine gun positions had been established by 52 Brigade Machine Gun Company.

On the right flank of the attack things did not go so well. Two assaulting companies of the 1st Royal Welsh Fusiliers advanced but more resistance was encountered in Quadrangle Trench. The left company of the 1st Royal Welsh Fusiliers got into the trench and

36

shortly after 2.00am linked with the 9th Northumberland Fusiliers on the left. They then started to bomb along the trench to the right where there was some more resistance. At 1.30am runners had reported that the right hand company was held up by the German wire where they were bombed and caught by the British artillery barrage falling short. The reserve company were waiting in Bottom Wood and at 2.00am half that company led by Lieutenant Dadd were called forward. Confusion was still reported and even more reinforcements were called up. Just then Lieutenant Dadd arrived back and reported that the trench had been cleared so further assistance was not required.

The 1st Royal Irish on the extreme right flank of the attack made an encouraging start and progressed through the wet and soggy conditions a distance of about 150 yards in ten minutes. They were then counter-attacked and driven back. The 1st Royal Welsh Fusiliers attempted to assist the 2nd Royal Irish to occupy Wood Trench by bombing along to the left in Quadrangle Trench towards Wood Trench but it was found that a gap existed between the end of Quadrangle Trench and Wood Trench which consisted of a small valley through which the light railway line ran and it was swept by machine gun fire. It was reported later that a patrol did get across this gap into Wood Trench and drove the Germans towards Mametz Wood, finally returning to Quadrangle Trench but the 2nd Royal Irish had already withdrawn by then. The officer leading that patrol was Second-Lieutenant S Sassoon and a rather different account of these exploits are better known:

> *There wasn't much wire in front of Quadrangle Trench. I entered it at a strong point on the extreme left and exploring to*

Typical light railway built by the British Army to move supplies on the Somme. TAYLOR LIBRARY

Route taken by Siegfried Sassoon when he 'attacked' Wood Trench which was situated about fifty yards behind the small bush.

the right I found young Fernby.

Kendle, who had been trying to do something for a badly wounded man, now rejoined me, and we continued, mostly on all fours, along the dwindling trench. The trench became a shallow groove and ended where the ground overlooked a little valley along which there was a light railway line. We stared across at the Wood. From the other side of the valley came an occasional rifle-shot, and a helmet bobbed up for a moment. The helmet bobbed up again. "I'll just have a shot at him" he said wriggling away from the crumbling bank which gave us cover. At this moment Fernby appeared with two men and a Lewis gun. Kendle

View from the position of the German held trench.

was half kneeling against some broken ground; I remember seeing him push his tin hat back from his forehead and then raise himself a few inches to take aim. After firing once he looked at us with a lively smile; a second later he fell sideways. A blotchy mark showed where the bullet had hit him just above the eyes.

The circumstances being what they were, I had no justification for feeling either shocked or astonished by the sudden extinction of Lance-Corporal Kendle. But after blank awareness that he was killed, all feelings tightened and contracted to a single intention – "to settle that sniper" on the other side of the valley. If I had stopped to think, I shouldn't have gone at all. As it was, I discarded my tin hat and equipment, slung a bag of bombs across my shoulder, abruptly informed Fernby that I was going to find out who was there, and set off at a downhill double. While I was running I pulled the safety-pin

*out of a Mills' bomb; my right hand being loaded, I did the same
for my left. I mention this because I was obliged to extract the
second safety-pin with my teeth, and the grating sensation
reminded me that I was half way across and not so reckless as I
had been when I started. I was even a little out of breath as I
trotted up the opposite slope. Just before I arrived at the top I
slowed up and threw my two bombs. Then I rushed at the bank,
vaguely expecting some sort of scuffle with my imagined enemy.
I had lost my temper with the man who had shot Kendle; quite
unexpectedly, I found myself looking down into a well-conducted
trench with a great many Germans in it. Fortunately for me, they
were already retreating. It had not occurred to them that they
were being attacked by a single fool; and Fernby, with presence
of mind which probably saved me, had covered my advance by
traversing the top of the trench with his Lewis gun. I slung a few
more bombs, but they fell short of the clumsy field-grey figures,
some of whom had turned to fire their rifles over the left shoulder
as they ran across the open toward the wood, while a crowd of
jostling helmets vanished along the trench.*

*Having thus failed to commit suicide, I proceeded to occupy
the trench – that is to say, I sat down on the fire-step, very much
out of breath, and hoped to God the Germans wouldn't come
back again.*

Sassoon then explored the empty trench in the direction of Mametz
Wood and according to Robert Graves writing in *Goodbye to All That*
sat down and read a book of poems. When he finally returned to
Bottom Wood he faced the wrath of Colonel Stockdale. His presence
in the enemy trench had held up an artillery bombardment for three
hours.

The 2nd Royal Irish Battalion war diary once again is extremely
detailed:

*'July 5. Our objective was Wood Trench and Mametz Wood.
This attack was commenced at 10.15pm under a heavy barrage
from our guns. C Coy under Capt Bell was ordered to attack
Wood Trench with A Coy in Support. The Grenade Coy under
Capt Gordon Ralph was again ordered to attack Strip Trench
with B Coy on the right to form a defensive flank. D Coy was kept
in Battalion reserve. The R. Welsh Fusiliers attacked on our left
their objective being Quadrangle Trench.*

*A rapid and dashing attack was made by all the Companies
concerned, C Coy reached the wire in front of Wood Trench in*

less than 10 minutes while the Grenade Coy again entered Strip Trench. The wire in front of Wood Trench was found by C Coy to be uncut and being extremely thick could not be penetrated. This Coy was exposed to a very heavy close-range fire and suffered severely, Capt Bell being killed on the German wire & two of his officers wounded.

July 5/6. C Coy was ordered to retire about 50 yards under cover of a fold in the ground and await reinforcements from A Coy which were brought up rapidly by Capt O'Reilly who took command of both Coys, Three times between midnight and dawn Capt O'Reilly attacked Wood Trench in a most gallant manner each time being only held up by the German wire which proved an insurmountable obstacle. The enemy's fire was intense and their trenches were very strongly held. At Dawn the commanding Officer ordered Capt O'Reilly to give it up and return which he was most reluctant to do although severely wounded in the hand. On our left the R Welsh. Fusrs entered the German trenches but were unable to bomb along to our assistance as the Quadrangle Trench did not join up with Wood Trench.

Meanwhile the Grenade Coy covered by B Coy were hammering away at Strip Trench and here fighting was almost entirely of a hand-to-hand nature. Capt Gordon Ralph was wounded in the neck but carried on until carried away unconscious. Lieut Pike who took command of the Grenade Coy led two attacks on Strip Trench and once again entered Mametz Wood only to be driven out by fierce bombing counter-attacks.

Capt Moore-Brabazon was wounded in the foot by an enemy bayonet and handed over command of B Coy to Lieut Blake who was blown up by a shell and carried away shortly after. Attack

Captain Gordon Ralph

Ground across which 2nd Royal Irish made rapid progress towards Wood Trench which was situated in middle distance. (See Map 5)

German snipers picked off unwary British soldiers, which hampered movement and trench repair work. This German sniper has himself being caught unawares. TAYLOR LIBRARY

after attack was made but progress was impossible and at about 3.30 am the Battalion was ordered by B.G.C. 22 Brigade to retire and return to Mansel Copse.

Our casualties in this attack were 125 all ranks. Capt Bell and Lieut White were killed, both inside the German wire; Capt Moore-Brabazon, Capt O'Reilly, Lieut Blake, Capt Gordon-Ralph, Lieut Price and C.S.M. Burns were wounded. The Chaplain, the Rev Fr Fitzmaurice distinguished himself by rescuing wounded under a heavy fire & R.S.M. Carew did very good work getting up ammunition under fire.'

Meanwhile the 1st Royal Welsh Fusiliers consolidated their positions in Quadrangle Trench and Lieutenant Dadd and Lieutenant Stevens led bombers and assault troops up Quadrangle Alley and established a 'stop' about halfway up to its junction with Quadrangle Support. Quadrangle Trench was repaired and deepened where it was very shallow on the right. Six Lewis gun emplacements were established in case of any counter-attack. As daylight came snipers in Mametz Wood became active and work had to be abandoned. Two counter-attacks were made by German bombers working down Quadrangle Alley to the 'stop', the first at dawn and another later in the morning. These were easily repulsed by the bombers and Lewis Gunners. Quadrangle Alley was quite shallow at that point and the heads of the Germans could be seen as they moved down the trench to the 'stop' which they were allowed to approach. They were then bombed and enfiladed by Lewis gunners from Quadrangle Trench and so both attacks were destroyed in this way. The 'stop' was then converted into a strong point and a further strong point established at the junction of Bottom Alley and Quadrangle Trench.

The 1st Royal Welsh Fusiliers had suffered sixty five casualties including eight killed in this operation. The Northumberland Fusiliers had a total of forty one casualties. The casualties of the 10th Lancashire Fusiliers were not disclosed.

Caterpillar Wood and Marlborough Copse Occupied

South-east of Mametz Wood the 18th Division held the sector on the right of the 7th Division.

18th Division

While the assault on Quadrangle Trench and Mametz Wood was taking place the 10th Essex (53 Brigade) already in position forward of Montauban Alley advanced at 2.52am. They found the approach trenches impassable and advanced over the open ground and entered Caterpillar Wood unopposed at 3.10am, in spite of reports from patrols that it was being held. Five enemy guns were captured and one machine gun was found. The 10th Essex were supposed to link up with the 2nd Royal Irish, so when they were not at the point arranged a lance corporal and one man pushed westwards to try and make contact. As we know the 2nd Royal Irish attack had failed and a hostile machine gun in the south-east corner of Mametz Wood opened fire and shot the two men as they made their patrol. The 10th Essex then moved across the valley to Marlborough Copse and finding it empty established a strong point.

At 12.30pm XV Corps ordered the 17th Division to attack Quadrangle Support Trench and Pearl Alley later that evening, in conjunction with an attack on the left by the 23rd Division. Major-

German machine gun teams.

General Pilcher was not happy about the position on his left in contact with 23rd Division. He wanted this strengthened and sent a message to XV Corps requesting that the 23rd Division take over a portion of the line as far east as Shelter Alley. He also wanted to know what the objective of the 23rd Division's attack was to be. When Pilcher's communication arrived at XV Corps HQ at 2.00pm Lieutenant-General Horne was in a meeting and the reply to Pilcher was inconclusive in as much as it refused his requests but stated that the attack would not take place unless the position on the left was strengthened. The 17th Division were ordered to establish a strong point at the point marking the divisional boundary on the Contalmaison road.

Horne returned at about 5 o'clock from his meeting at Army Headquarters and the apparent uncertainty on how to proceed was ended when he brought with him new draft orders. At 9.30pm Pilcher and Major-General I Phillips commanding the 38th Welsh Division travelled to Heilly for a meeting with Horne at which plans for an attack on Mametz Wood were discussed and draft orders were issued. In preparation for this attack there was a reorganisation of the divisional boundaries. Pilcher's concerns about his left flank were resolved as the 23rd Division were to move to the east of Shelter Alley as he originally requested.

The 38th Division Come Into The Line

The relief of the 7th Division by the 38th Division who had Headquarters at Grovetown commenced and the divisional boundaries were also adjusted on the right. Among those of the 7th Division being relieved was Second-Lieutenant Siegfried Sassoon and he recorded his impressions of the occasion later, with a premonition of their ultimate destiny.

'They were mostly undersized men and as I watched them arriving at the first stage of their battle experience I had a sense of their victimisation. A little platoon officer was settling his men down with a valiant show of self-assurance. For the sake of appearances orders of some kind had to be given though in reality there was nothing to do except sit down and hope it wouldn't rain. He spoke sharply to some of them, and I felt that they were like a lot of children. It was going to be a bad look-out for two such bewildered companies, huddled up in the Quadrangle, which had been over-garrisoned by our own comparatively small contingent. Visualising that forlorn crowd of

*khaki figures under the twilight of the trees, I can believe that I
saw then, for the first time, how blindly war destroys its victims.
The sun had gone down on my own reckless brandishings, and I
understood the doomed condition of these half trained civilians
who had been sent up to attack the Wood.'*

It was for the Welshmen an inauspicious introduction to the Battle of
the Somme. Captain Glynn Jones, 14th Royal Welsh Fusiliers, writing
after the war, also recalled the same occasion:-

*'With darkness came guides – at any rate they were called
such from the 1st Battalion, and my company was instructed to
relieve another in a trench known as Quadrangle Trench, which
lay about 500 yards west of Mametz Wood. Apparently this trench
had only been taken that morning, as we found to our cost when
we got there.*

*Our guides lost their way, but having wandered over most of
the country we found ourselves in a half dug trench and we were
told that "this was the spot". By now I can forgive the company
of the 1st Battalion for the unseemly haste with which it
departed, but at the time coming from an area where reliefs had
amounted almost to a ceremonial parade, I was little less than
amazed when I found no officers, no instructions, no
information, or anything else, and found that the tired regulars
had departed almost as quickly as the Portuguese used to up
north.*

*In any case we put out our men as far as we could. We found
that about 200yds to our right, the same trench[1] was still
occupied by Germans, and a bombing post at this end and
another up an old communication trench going forward [2] were
among our early operations of defence.*

*Later with the help of bombs we tried to penetrate further in
these directions but found them to be strongly occupied. So
having posted our sentries we spent the night slinging dead over
the parapet and deeping our trench. We spent two days in the
most miserable conditions in this trench. But apart from a
number of casualties through enemy shelling, short rations, and
mud, we did not do badly. In fact we had a great deal of fun
"potting" at Germans on the edge of Mametz Wood to our right
and also in our own trench where it dipped into the hollow
between us and that wood. But it was indeed a relief to be
relieved on the night of the 7th I believe and to receive
instructions to collect at Fricourt. But getting to Fricourt was*

another matter, and, as far as my army days go I am ashamed of nothing so much as the route along which I dragged my poor company to rendezvous. But considering the maze of old trenches, wire and darkness, and a severe shelling near Shelter Wood I can now well wonder that we even got to Fricourt at all.'

1. [Wood Trench]
2. [Quadrangle Alley]

The 8th South Staffordshires had remained in support to the attack of 52 Brigade all day. As the 9th Northumberland Fusiliers occupied Quadrangle Trench so the A and B Companies moved into the Hedge Line Trench where they remained all day under shell fire. They were finally relieved in the evening. As they were leaving Railway Copse a shell landed directly on B Company killing twenty men and wounding many others.

Dear Wife

In answer to your kind and welcome letter and was very sorry to hear that little Florrie was very bad again. Dear wife, I have asked you to send me a wire if she was getting not better and then I might get a pass to come over and see you and the children.

Wife, I don't know who that man can be but if he comes up again ask him his name and let me know in your next letter.

Dear wife, I am not quite teetotal but I don't have a lot now as I find it has done me not good but you know yourself as I could not give it up altogether. Dear wife, they want me to take the Stripes but I shall not take them as I suffer too much with my chest and you have got to do a lot of shouting and it might play me up again and I think I have had enough illness since I have been out here so I am going to look after myself so as I can work for you and my children.

When I get home again and I hope it will soon be over so we can be together again and enjoy ourselfs once more. Dear wife, I have not received any letter from our Arthur but he might write if he is going out to the front as you say. And I hope he has luck to come back again and tell Alf and Jennie I wish them good luck and I hope he has not got to go out again as once is enough and tell him to keep away from here if he can as it is a rotten place for Duty as you never know when you are finished and I hope to see him very shortly all being well and have a jolly time together once again. So I think this is all this time so Good Night and God Bless you and the children with best love.

xxxxxxxxxxxxxxxxxxxxxxxxxxxxxxxxxxxxxxxxxxx xxxxxx

From Husband to Wife with Best Love xxxxxxxxxxxxxx

Pleas answer straight back and don't forget to let me know how little Florrie is if she is no better send a Wire at once.

A member of the ill fated B Company was Private George Hawkins of Walsall who was in the Territorial Army in August 1914 having previously fought in the Boer War in South Africa. He was aged thirty four and was married to Florence. They had four children, one of whom was also called Florence. He had been in France since July 1915 and had previously written to his wife before being killed.

THE WELSH ARMY

With the outbreak of war in August 1914 plans were put in hand almost immediately to augment the strength of the British regular and territorial army.

Lord Kitchener who had been appointed Secretary of State for War appeared on posters throughout the land with his now familiar pointing finger exclaiming 'Your Country Needs You'. The effect was immediate and the recruiting offices were soon overwhelmed by the numbers of young men clamouring to sign up for the 'King's Shilling' which was the amount payable on enlistment. By the end of August, Lord Derby had introduced the idea of raising battalions from within existing communities and thus encouraged friends, workmates, sports organisations and youth organisations, indeed any kind of group to join up together and so bring with them an already established indigenous sense of comradeship into the new battalion. As examples, the 16th Royal Welsh Fusiliers were originally recruited from employees at the City Hall in Cardiff and the first thousand recruits wore the badge the Cardiff City coat of arms. The 10th and 13th Welsh were recruited from the mining areas and became known as the 1st and 2nd Rhondda. The 14th Welsh owe their existence to the Swansea Cricket and Football Club. Interestingly the 15th Welsh had well over three hundred recruits from Bolton in Lancashire and were known as the 15th Carmarthenshire.

It was David Lloyd George who was Chancellor of the Exchequer of the then Liberal Government of the time who proposed to recruit and form a Welsh Army of two divisions. The idea went ahead but recruitment was slow and the intended target of the first 50,000 seemed a long way off as many Welshmen had already responded and joined in other regiments. It was some twelve months later before the target figure was

47

reached. The idea of a second division was then abandoned. Having created a Welsh Army the problem of how to lead it presented itself. There was a general shortage of officers in all of Kitchener's 'new' armies, and many officers were brought out of retirement and some of these had only limited experience. The 'political' dimension created by the decision of the Chancellor to involve himself in a personal recruitment of a Welsh Army was heightened when a number of the senior officers were appointed through the influence of David Lloyd George.

**38th
Division**

The men of the 38th (Welsh) Division who arrived on the Somme had come marching south from their initiation in the trenches during the early months of 1916 further to the north. Marching for a week, contemporary reports describe them as being tired and footsore on their arrival.

38th Division at camp.

Chapter Four

TOMORROW WE MUST GO TO TAKE SOME CURSED WOOD
6 July

The weather showed no signs of improvement, the wind strengthened and there was intermittent rain. The newly captured British Front line positions were consolidated during the day. The Germans did not make any counter-attack but continued to shell the British positions. The British artillery replied putting down a barrage on Quadrangle Support Trench and Pearl Alley which was reported to be full of Germans.

At about four o'clock in the afternoon it was reported that four machine guns had been hit by shellfire at the southern corner of Shelter Wood. Lieutenant Stanbury set out from Fricourt Chateau with a rescue team. When he arrived he found three men already dead and the wounded still under shellfire. Some of the wounded were buried and frantic work commenced to dig them out. Private Straffon worked exceptionally digging down four feet with only his entrenching tool to rescue Private Coombes. In all there were three men killed Sergeant Taylor, Private Gibbs and Private Gibson and five others wounded in this incident who were all then successfully evacuated.

At 10.00am an order had been issued by XV Corps for attacks on Pearl Alley, Quadrangle Support Trench and Mametz Wood for 7 July. The orders were long and detailed and proposed a joint attack to be undertaken by the 17th and 38th Division on Mametz Wood.

The objective of the 38th Welsh Division was to attack the wood from the east and enter the wood at the 'Hammerhead', so called because of its shape, and push forward towards the centre and meet up with units of the 17th Division who would similarly attack the wood from the west. Both divisions were then to push northwards to the northern edge of the wood.

The co-ordination of this movement was to be ensured by a preliminary attack on Quadrangle Support Trench which would clear the way for the 17th Division to attack the wood which, unlike the eastern side, was still defended at its western approaches. It was still intended, however, to go ahead with the main attack even if this preliminary attack failed. With an amended timetable this trench would simply become the first objective of the units who were to move into Mametz Wood and meet up with the 38th Division. In addition the 17th Division were to send in units to clear up Strip Trench, Wood Trench, and Wood Support Trench and sweep the southern end of Mametz Wood in conjunction with a unit of the 38th Division who would enter the wood at its southern tip.

The preliminary attack at 2.00am was to be made by 52 Brigade but Major-General Pilcher was not convinced that the trenches could be taken and argued without success that an isolated attack subject to enfilade machine gun attack from Contalmaison on the left and Mametz Wood on the right could not succeed. XV Corps argument in proposing this attack plan was that if these trenches were taken then the planned attacks on Contalmaison and Mametz Wood would then be made much easier.

The attack of 52 Brigade was again to be entrusted to the 9th Northumberland Fusiliers and the 10th Lancashire Fusiliers who had not suffered severely in their successful attack on Quadrangle Trench on 5 July.

7 July

At midnight on 6/7 July the assaulting companies moved up into Quadrangle Trench. The 9th Northumberland Fusiliers were on the right of the attack up to the block in Quadrangle Alley. The 10th Lancashire Fusiliers were on the left near Shelter Alley. In support was the 9th Duke of Wellingtons Regiment.

A bombardment of twenty five minutes preceded the attack but, at 1.10am, all communication was lost with the attacking troops. At 3.15am a runner of the 9th Northumberland Fusiliers reported that the leading waves of the attack had failed to reach their objective and this

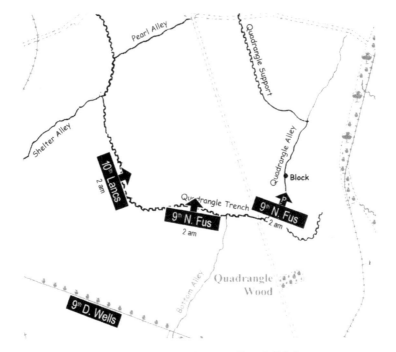

Map 6. First attack on Quadrangle Support Trench 7 July.

was followed by a lamp signal message that the attack was hampered by uncut wire in front of Quadrangle Support Trench. In addition many British shells fell very short of the German lines. The troops were then met by the Germans who themselves were preparing to attack. An elite corps of the 2nd Division of the Prussian Guard left their trenches and advancing downhill met their attackers head on in No Man's Land.

The 10th Lancashire Fusiliers, similarly, were immediately met with intense machine gun and rifle fire and were driven back. The two left companies however eventually got a foothold in Pearl Alley which was shallow and lightly held and pushed up towards Contalmaison. Supporting the attack of the 10th Lancashire Fusiliers was Lieutenant Stanbury leading gun crews of 52 Brigade Machine Gun Company who with the left companies of the Fusiliers fought up Pearl Alley with two gun crews. A platoon of the Fusiliers came under heavy attack in No Man's Land. Private Cocks of 52 Brigade Machine Gun Corps went to their assistance, leaving the cover of Pearl Alley and taking his gun into the open and firing on the attackers and driving them back. Attacked again on the other flank he opened fire again and only retired when the enemy approached to within about fifty yards.

By 3.00am Sergeant Smith returned to Quadrangle Trench and reported he had left Lieutenant Stanbury lying out in No Man's Land. He had been with him on the parapet of Quadrangle Support Trench when a shell fragment hit him in the left leg, virtually severing it below the knee. Sergeant Smith dragged him back into the cover of a shell hole where a stretcher bearer of the 9th Duke of Wellingtons bandaged him up. The area continued to be heavily shelled but at 4.00am Second-Lieutenant Michell led a patrol forward in broad daylight to search for Lieutenant Stanbury at the spot where he was left by Sergeant Smith to bring him in. Despite all their efforts, searching all shell holes in the area, no trace of him could be found and he was reported missing. The Fusiliers held on until daybreak when they were forced to retire to Quadrangle Trench by a German counter attack.

In the event of the preliminary attack on Quadrangle Trench failing the orders were to continue with the main assault as planned but with an amended timetable which allowed the artillery to bombard the German positions for a further thirty minutes than originally planned. The original bombardment was to commence at 7.20am and continue until 8.00am and a further thirty minutes should mean that it would lift at 8.30am. However XV Corps issued orders at 5.25am to attack Quadrangle Support again at 8.00am. The confusion over the orders for the timing of the attack and the congestion in the trenches, especially on the left where the 23rd Division were taking over Shelter Alley and part of Quadrangle Trench left insufficient time for preparation.

The battalions involved in the second attack were the 9th Duke of Wellingtons and the 12th Manchesters. The telephone lines had still not been restored and in Quadrangle Trench the 9th Northumberland Fusiliers did not receive orders until 7.00am for relief by the 12th Manchesters who although due to attack at 8.00am were still in Fricourt at 7.00am. Similarly on the left only two companies of the 9th Duke of Wellingtons were able to get forward and replace the 10th Lancashire Fusiliers having only received their orders at 7.25am. It was 7.45am before the 12th Manchesters reached Bottom Wood and the Hedgeline. They advanced towards Quadrangle Trench and without pausing passed through the 9th Northumberland Fusiliers still in Quadrangle Trench and advanced towards their objective, some 500 yards distant. The leading battle patrols arrived at their point of attack some minutes late. The artillery barrage had lifted by then and advancing in broad daylight and left without the protection of its own artillery the assaulting troops of were cut down by machine gun fire mainly from Mametz Wood. Small parties did penetrate as far as Acid Drop Copse but casualties were extremely heavy. The Manchesters suffered sixteen of their officers killed or wounded and similarly 529 other ranks.

The 9th Duke of Wellingtons on the left attempted to re-take Pearl Alley and bombed their way forward to the Cemetery led by Captain Benjamin with Company Sergeant-Major Green at his side. A very violent bombardment was opened by the Germans causing heavy casualties and a heavy counter-attack from Quadrangle Support Trench forced them back. Attacking in lesser numbers than the 12th Manchesters the 9th Duke of Wellingtons casualties were fourteen officers and 251 other ranks.

Captain Benjamin

The showery conditions gave way in the afternoon of the 7th to incessant rain. The whole area was turning into a vast swamp, trenches were collapsing, clinging mud in places up to waist deep made any movement extremely difficult and exhausting. Amid these conditions the occupants of Quadrangle Trench were ragged and disorganised. The 9th Northumberland Fusiliers having been withdrawn to Bottom Wood and the Hedgeline were soon ordered forward again and shortly after 11.00am were back in Quadrangle Trench with four machine gun positions established. However at 11.20am

Company Sergeant-Major Green

the 10th Sherwood Foresters also received orders to occupy Quadrangle Trench and arrived at 12.15pm. They found it occupied by 'representatives of three battalions' and unable to squeeze any more than two companies into the trench. The confusion was further added to because the Germans in counter-attacking Contalmaison had forced troops of the neighbouring 23rd Division down the left hand side of Quadrangle Trench and into the 17th Division sector. There were only limited telephone communications and special liaison officers were organising runners to establish contact between the battalions at the

Attacking British infantry being encouraged by their officer. Inset: badge of Manchester Regiment found recently on the battlefield.

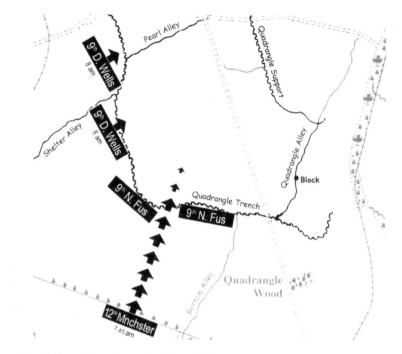

Map 7. Second attack on Quadrangle Support Trench 7 July.

front, brigades and divisional headquarters.

At 12.20pm Lieutenant Colonel E G Harrison, Commanding Officer of the 12th Manchesters, arrived with orders to clear up the situation and organise an attack. Soon afterwards though, Harrison was wounded and had an amazing escape. He was shot through the neck, the bullet missing the spinal cord and main arteries. After having his wound dressed he was able to make his way through Bottom Wood and a hail of shells to Brigade Headquarters where, though shaken and exhausted, he was able to give a report.

Lieutenant Colonel H Bryan was placed in command and after consulting Lieutenant Colonel Clive (7th East Yorks) and Captain Duval, now commanding the 12th Manchesters reported at 2.00pm to Brigade Headquarters and consequently the third attack was cancelled. At 4.15pm all units of 52 Brigade were ordered to withdraw. The remnants of the 9th Northumberland Fusiliers then retired with the 10th Manchesters and 9th Duke of Wellingtons and by 6.00pm marched from Fricourt in the pouring rain to Meaulte. During the period 4-7 July the 9th Northumberland Fusiliers casualties amounted to fourteen officers and 299 other ranks.

On the right hand of the 17th Division sector the result of the preliminary attack at 2.00am on 7 July was awaited in the early hours by the 7th East Yorks and 6th Dorsets. Their attack on the south-west

54

approaches of Mametz Wood depended on the   preliminary attack successfully capturing the junction of Quadrangle Support and Quadrangle Alley. Failure to achieve this would result in any attack on the Wood being subject to close range enemy fire from the left flank and rear from this position.

At 7.30am the news came through that the preliminary attack had failed. Initially it was proposed to go ahead with the whole of the original attack ordered. Major G C King, Commanding the 7th East Yorks, persuaded the Brigadier in extended telephone conversations to make the main attack dependent on successful bombing attacks on the junction of Quadrangle Support and Quadrangle Alley and so avoid this crossfire. The outcome of this venture is recorded in the report of

to the...:

Comdg Officer 7th East Yorks.

Referring to the attack by two platoons of B. Coy. on the junction of Quad Support + Quad Alley by moving at across the open + jumping into the enemies trench + proceed to Bomb. We had to cross 50yds of open ground which was being swept by M Guns & when within 15 yds of our objective I found I had only 4 men with me + there I got in to the end of our trench + was later joined by the officer leading the attack, Lieutenant L Holroyd.

Lieutenant Holroyd was unable to reach the German trench as they had constructed a large 'block' about twenty yards from the junction of the two trenches. At 10.15am Major King sent the following message

'Bombed up Quad Alley as far as Quad Support which is held
by the enemy. Unable to dislodge him I am holding Quad Alley
and Quad Trench. Enemy holding strip of wood down railway
and Quad Support. Awaiting Instructions. '

The operation had resulted in sixteen killed in action, numbers of wounded were undisclosed and it still left any further attacks exposed to enfilade fire from that part of Quadrangle Alley held by the

6 more the whole party included 3 bombers. I at once arranged these into a bombing squad with what bombs we had, I could not see how I was to bomb two trenches with these few men, ~~I wanted~~ so I proceeded to find out how the corner was held, so we advanced down the trench & came across a barrier, two men crossed this stop when the Hun bombed us back. (Bagley + Cpl. Farr). I could see the Hun trench going to the Left + to the front, we had lost two men before this

by rifle fire from directly in front
& I had sent me back as
messenger, which left 6 men
as the Hun was throwing
further than we could & down
hill at that; I looked for
rifle grenades & we had none
So I decided not to go
forward, until I got more
men up. when the order
came up for us to fall back.

L. Holroyd. Lt
B. Coy.

Lieutenant Lister Holroyd

Germans.

During the afternoon conflicting reports circulated about the situation in Quadrangle Support Trench. Some erroneous messages had been sent back stating that it was in British hands. At 2.10pm XV Corps issued orders for a new attack.

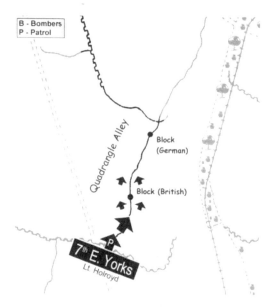

Map 8. Lieutenant Holroyd's attack on the German 'block'.

Zero hour was to be 5.00pm. The 50th Brigade, the 7th East Yorks and 6th Dorsets on the right were to advance on the western side of Mametz Wood and capture Wood Trench and the long strip of wood through which the railway ran. 51 Brigade with the 10th Sherwood Foresters were to make a third attack on Quadrangle Support Trench. There was much discussion on the telephone with XV Corps Headquarters regarding the actual situation in Quadrangle Support. This being inconclusive Lieutenant General Horne was obliged at 4.05pm to cancel this proposed assault.

Meanwhile in the trenches occupied by the 7th East Yorks the original orders to attack at 5.00pm had been confirmed. At 4.20pm the orders for cancellation arrived at Battalion Headquarters but by then Major King was in the front line intending to lead 'B' Company himself whose officers had all been wounded. Two runners set off and finding the trenches blocked ran over the top and somehow managed to reach Major King at 4.58pm, just in time to halt the lone advance.

At 6.10pm the cancelled attack was reinstated to take place at 8.00pm after a bombardment commencing at 7.30pm.

The Welsh at the Hammerhead

The tasks allotted to the 38th Welsh Division were in turn passed to 115 Brigade which was commanded by Brigadier-General H J Evans.

During the morning of 6 July Evans reconnoitred the ground over which the attack was to be made. A long, narrow, winding valley runs down the northern face of Caterpillar Wood which provided some cover for attacking troops in addition to that provided by the wood itself, Further north, though, on the ridge above the valley the troops would be very exposed not only to frontal fire from the edge of Mametz Wood but from the right hand side where the German lines ran parallel to the direction of the attack and where there were certain to be machine gun posts dug in. Evan's plan was to attack with two battalions, but he decided not to have any troops on the exposed ridge. Instead he proposed to attack on a single battalion frontage in the more sheltered valley, with the second battalion following the leading battalion into the attack. Another was to be in support in Caterpillar Wood and a fourth in reserve further back. Accordingly he put arrangements in hand to proceed on that basis.

When news of the formation was received at XV Corps Headquarters a message was sent to 38th Division Headquarters at Grovetown that no more than two battalions should be assembled in the western end of Caterpillar Wood and the valley as this would cause overcrowding and with it the risk of high casualties from shell fire '..... two battalions are considered sufficient for the attack on the eastern projection of the wood with a third in support in Montauban Alley and a fourth further back' it concluded.

Evans was dismayed but had no alternative but to set about issuing revised orders for the attack which was due at 8.30am the next morning. It was 2.00am before he was able to send the revised orders to the battalion commanders concerned. Evans then made his way to

The Red Dragon getting the better of the Imperial German Eagle. A card sold to raise funds for soldiers and sailors from the town of Llandilo.

Caterpillar Wood to help re-organise the battalions which were now to attack on a two battalion frontage.

The disposition for the attack placed the 11th South Wales Borderers on the left near the edge of Caterpillar Wood and the 16th

59

Welsh on the right on the ridge above the valley, the whole width of the attack being about 500 yards. The 10th South Wales Borderers were to be in reserve in Montauban Alley.

It is not clear why Evans came to change the frontage of the attack from one battalion to a two battalion frontage. The message from XV Corps ordering the withdrawal of two battalions from the immediate area of the attack, passed on by 38th Division Headquarters made no comment or recommendation on the proposed width of the attack, only the number of battalions to be involved. It could be of course, that Evans, in his frustration made verbal contact with 38th Division Headquarters and subsequently received a verbal response about this matter which has not been recorded.

Attached to 115 Brigade Headquarters' staff at that time was a young officer by the name of Captain Wyn Griffith. Some years later Griffith was to write of his experiences at Mametz Wood in that Great War Classic *Up to Mametz*.

Griffith was preparing to move early on 7 July to Pommiers Redoubt where Brigade Headquarters was to be established for the forthcoming attack. He had spent the night in an old German dugout and awaking at 4.30am he went up into the trench above to have a look around. Returning to the dugout he found Lieutenant Taylor the brigade signalling officer who had been out all night putting down telephone wires to Pommiers Redoubt. Eventually they set off together along Danzig Alley to make the journey to the new headquarters. On the way Griffith confided in Taylor that he was worried about his younger brother Watcyn whom he had not seen for some days.

Captain Wyn Griffith

'He's such a kid, for all his uniform. He ought to be still in school, not in this bloody shambles.'

'He's all right' replied Taylor. 'I saw him last night. The brigade called for two runners from each battalion and he came as one of them, he's somewhere near that old German dugout we came from.'

'I wish I'd known; it was his birthday two days ago and I've got a little present for him in my valise. I wonder if he'll see another birthday?'

The Brigade Headquarters had good views of Mametz Wood itself but the area from which the battalions were to attack was hidden from view. Soon after the British artillery commenced their bombardment at 8.00am, the German artillery response cut

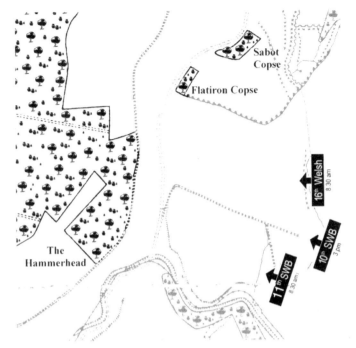

Map 9. 38th Welsh Division's attack on the 'Hammerhead' 7 July.

communication between the Brigade Headquarters and the attacking troops. The assault however got under way on time, at 8.30am, attacking the Hammerhead which was defended by 11/Lehr Regiment (3rd German Division) and the 11/163rd Regiment. As soon as the leading waves of the 16th Welsh came over the crest of the slope they were hit by heavy frontal machine gun fire from the Hammerhead and enfilade fire from Flat Iron Copse and Sabot Copse on their right. It had been intended to place a smoke screen barrage on the right of the attack to protect the 16th Welsh against enfilade fire from the copses but it never appeared. Major Angus of the 16th Welsh personally directed every attempt to get forward showing a fine example of leadership and disregard of danger by constantly exposing himself to fire.

Major Angus

Captain Williams of C Company was also prominent among the officers leading the attack of the 16th Welsh but he was badly wounded coming over the ridge.

Company Sergeant Major Thomas was lying close to the ground alongside his company commander, Captain Hardman. He attempted to move forward and raised himself up but was immediately shot through the head.

Among the other officers of the 16th Welsh that day were two

61

brothers Lieutenants Arthur and Leonard Tregaskis who had joined the 38th Division on the same day, were promoted Corporal on the same day and later commissioned on the same day. They were also to die together, on the same day. Eye witness reports stated that as one brother fell mortally wounded so the other was killed going to his assistance.

They were not the only brothers from the battalion to die that day. Private Henry Morgan and his younger brother Private Charles Morgan both of A Company enlisted together in Cardiff and died together.

Two other brothers were also serving in the 16th Welsh and both were to die in Mametz Wood. Private Albert Oliver died on 7 July while his brother Ernest was only to outlive him by three days being killed on the 10 July.

On the left the 11th South Wales Borderers pushed forward through the valley but were also driven back by intense frontal machine gun fire from the Hammerhead. Several officers immeditely became casualties including the Adjutant Lieutenant Pryce-Hamer.

Lieutenant T Pryce-Hamer who played Association Football for Wales.

Back at Brigade Headquarters, Evans sent Captain Hinton from Brigade Headquarters to Caterpillar Wood at 8.45am to send back early information. However, at 10.00am messages were first received from the attacking battalions that the attack was temporarily held up by heavy machine gun fire. Ten minutes later Captain Hinton's first report arrived and confirmed that heavy rifle and machine gun fire had held up the attack 200 yards from the objective on the right flank (16th Welsh) and about 400 yards on the left flank (11th South Wales Borderers), casualties did not appear to be heavy and supplies of ammunition and grenades were being maintained.

Further artillery support was called for and more machine guns were pushed forward into Caterpillar Wood to try and fire northwards up the valley to counteract the enfilade fire of the German machine guns in the two copses.

The initial response from XV Corps to the message received at 10.10am for more artillery support was not sympathetic. The 38th Division were told to "continue the fight keeping the situation in their own hands" and to get support of the Divisional Artillery at Treux. They were also warned that the two battalions that "were alone engaged were sufficient for the task in hand" and not to throw any more men into the fight. XV Corps for some reason had a change of heart about the barrage and at 10.20am informed 38th Division that there would be a barrage by the heavy artillery on the eastern edge of Mametz Wood. This would commence at 10.45am and continue until

The Tregaskis Brothers. At the outbreak of war both brothers were farming in Canada and returned to Wales to enlist. They were promoted Lance Corporal on the same day and later they were commissioned on the same day. An eye witness said that as one brother was wounded so the other went to assist and he was also hit – they died together. Their father, a director of Spillers Nephews, later left Wales to live in the Channel Islands.

The village of Montauban and the hollow behind Marlborough Copse and the ground over which 115 Brigade battalions assembled.

Captured German position at Pommiers Redoubt, it became the HQ of 114 Brigade. (See Map 9)

11.15am. This information was immediately dispatched by runners to the assaulting battalions with instructions to dig in and make a further attack after the bombardment had been completed.

With apparent disregard for XV Corps instructions Brigadier General Evans sent for the Commanding Officer of the 10th South Wales Borderers to receive orders to move up his battalion, which was in support, in readiness to join the attack. Two companies of the 10th South Wales Borderers were ordered up and they were to be reinforced by the remaining two companies. Lieutenant Colonel S J Wilkinson commanding the battalion was instructed to press home the attack 'with vigour'.

The artillery bombardment commenced as planned but when telephone comm-unications were restored soon after 11.00am and the Commanding Officer of 16th Welsh was able to notify Brigade Headquarters that some shells were falling short and on to the British position which was at that time about 300 yards short of the wood.

During the early part of the afternoon casualties continued to mount and Brigadier General Evan's decision to involve the 10th South Wales Borderers was well founded. The heavy rain made conditions very difficult and the 10th South Wales Borderers made slow progress towards the front line.

Eventually a renewed attack was launched and following his orders Lieutenant Colonel Wilkinson endeavoured to press home this second assault and was in the second wave of attacking troops of his battalion

64

when he fell wounded. The attack gained nothing and was no nearer the Hammerhead than at the outset. Many officers had become casualties, now estimated to be in the region of 400 in total. Brigadier General Evans decided to leave Brigade Headquarters and go down to Caterpillar Wood to assess the situation for himself, telephone lines having again been cut. As he was about to leave just after 4.00pm orders came through from Divisional Headquarters to renew the attack at 5.00pm. Prior to that an artillery bombardment would take place at 4.30pm. Evans accompanied by Captain Griffith did not arrive at Caterpillar Wood until twenty minutes before the attack was due to take place and found the attacking battalion no closer to the wood than 250 yards 'partially dug in and somewhat disorganised'.

Captain J L Williams, Captain of the Welsh Rugby team, also played for the British Lions. Worked as a clerk in the Cardiff Coal Exchange. His ability to speak fluent French assisted in his promotion after joining the ranks of the Royal Fusiliers in 1914.

Griffith writing later observed that

> 'men were burrowing into the ground with their entrenching tools seeking whatever cover they might take . . . . . wounded men were crawling back from the ridge, men were crawling forward with ammunition. No attack could succeed over such ground as this swept from the front and side by machine guns at short range.'

On the way down, near Caterpillar Wood, Griffith spoke with an artillery officer who had a telephone that was still working. When they arrived at Queen's Nullah where there was an advanced dressing station they found scores of wounded men crowded under the protective bank out of sight of the enemy but very exposed to possible artillery bombardment.

Reluctantly Evans started to re-organise the troops and the positions of the machine guns and trench mortars. By 5.15pm this had only been partially completed. He had always had doubts about the viability of making an attack in daylight over

Company Sergeant Major 'Dick' Thomas. Member of the Glamorgan Constabulary, joined up in 1914 but was retained for police duties until January 1915. He was a Welsh Rugby International.

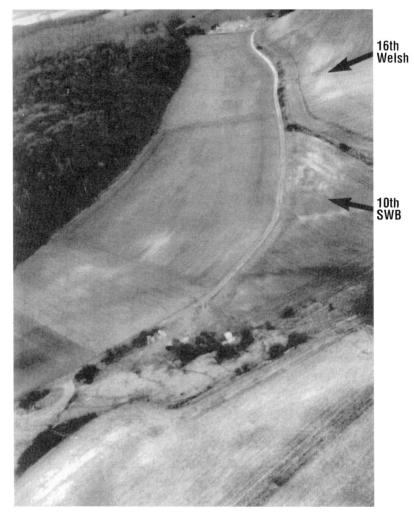

16th
Welsh

10th
SWB

View of the area in front of the 'Hammerhead' where many of the attackers were pinned down by German machine gunners. See Map 9

such ground and had favoured a surprise attack by creeping up to the edge of the wood in the dark and rushing it at first light. Griffith remembered the telephone he had seen near Caterpillar Wood and went to check if it was still working. Running back again to Queen's Nullah he found the General and guided him to the trench from where Evans contacted Division and argued with determination for a postponement of the attack, especially as by the time the troops could be organised properly the effect of the bombardment would have worn off.

It is not difficult to imagine the atmosphere at XV Corps Headquarters in Heilly. At about the same time 38th Division were passing Brigadier General Evans comments back there was similar confusion on the western side of Mametz Wood in the 17th Division sector where no-one could establish whether Quadrangle Support Trench had been captured or not. As we have seen the proposed attack by the 17th Division also to be at 5.00pm, was cancelled.

By 6.40pm the delayed 5.00pm attack by the 38th Division was also called off. To ensure safe delivery of the orders Evans and Griffith returned to Queen's Nullah by different routes. On the way back to Pommiers Redoubt the General confided in Griffith.

> *'I spoke my mind about the whole business . . . . . you heard me. They wanted us to press on at all costs, talked about determination, and suggested that I didn't realise the importance of the operation. As good as told me that I was tired and didn't want to tackle the job. Difficult to judge on the spot, they said! As if the whole trouble hadn't arisen because someone found it so easy to judge when he was six miles away and had never seen the country, and couldn't read a map. You mark my*

Frank James King DSM, 48068 RAMC 130th (St Johns Field Ambulance) 38th Division. took many wounded out of No Man's Land on the 7th July 1916.

Queen's Nullah was in constant use throughout the battle. Along this banking was an advanced dressing station, trench mortar positions and was later used as both battalion and brigade headquarters.

words they'll send me home for this: they want butchers not brigadiers. They'll remember now that I told them, before we began, that the attack could not succeed unless the machine guns were masked. I shall be in England in a month.'

Evan's opinion about the deadly effect of machine gun fire had been shared by his Divisional Commander, Major-General Phillips, who is reported to have given instructions to 115 Brigade to the effect that if any machine gun fire was experienced while advancing against Mametz Wood the Brigade was not to try and push home its attack but to return to its starting point and await another bombardment of the wood.

That night two companies of the 17th Royal Welsh Fusiliers moved up to hold the line opposite the Hammerhead while the three depleted and exhausted attacking battalions were withdrawn having suffered a total of over 400 casualties.

17th Division's Third Attempt on Quadrangle Support Trench

We can now return to events during the evening of the 7 July on the western side of the Wood where, it will be recalled Major King was about to lead his men into an assault when he received orders with two minutes to spare telling him the operation had been cancelled.

As we have seen the proposed attacks at 5.00pm by both divisions were cancelled but while the 38th Division was withdrawn the 17th Division were told to prepare for a third assault on Quadrangle Support Trench. The instructions issued to the 38th Division were to make a raid on Strip Trench that night and at daylight to push on and join up Strip Trench and Cliff Trench.

Although it had stopped raining in the late afternoon the ground was exceptionally heavy and made any movement extremely difficult. Reports of water and mud up to the waist were still reported from more than one source.

The attacking battalions were to be the 6th Dorsets on the right, the 7th East Yorks in the centre and the 10th Sherwood Foresters on the left. The assault was to be led by the bombers of the battalions concerned but was again going to be made alone with no advance being made by the division on the right against Contalmaison. On the right of the 6th Dorsets were the 15th Royal Welsh Fusiliers who had been waiting in Cliff Trench all day to exploit any success of the 38th Division assault on the Wood, with instructions to clear up the southern portion of the Wood.

The attack was timed to commence at 8.00pm in daylight. After a

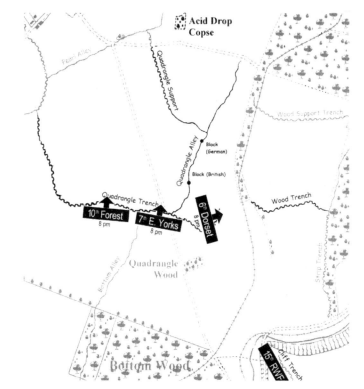

Map 10. Third attempt on Quadrangle Support Trench and Wood Trench 7 July.

bombardment lasting half an hour, the Sherwood Foresters attacked over the open but could not get nearer than forty yards to Quadrangle Support because of severe rifle and machine gun fire. Communications were cut by the enemy barrage which also fell on the advancing troops. A similar fate befell the 7th East Yorks who again assaulted the 'block' south of the junction between Quadrangle Alley and Quadrangle Support in an attempt to force their way up the valley carrying the railway line to the south west corner of Mametz Wood.

Approximate position from which Brigadier General Price Davies observed the 6th Dorsets attacking Strip Trench.

The 6th Dorsets were to attack Wood Trench with one company and the battalion bombers and expected support from the 15th Royal Welsh Fusiliers whom they had been told were to attack Strip Trench on their right. Leading the attack was Second- Lieutenant Albertanson. They were immediately fired on from three different directions and were decimated. Second-Lieutenant Albertanson, managed to struggle back with only three men in time to prevent a further company being sent in, thereby saving many lives, The Commanding Officer, Lieutenant Colonel L A Rowley seeing that there was no co-operation whatever on the right decided not to commit another company and they retired.

The 15th Royal Welsh Fusiliers had seemed unaware that their raid on Strip Trench was part of a much larger operation only sent in a patrol led by Lieutenant A Jones. It was described in the diary as a 'small operation . . . . . not pushed as the enemy suddenly revealed his strength in machine guns which crossed the approach to the wood. ' In the operation they suffered twelve casualties.

Brigadier-General L A E Price-Davies commanding 113 Brigade was at that time visiting the position held by the 15th Royal Welsh Fusiliers and writing later stated that he had never heard about this proposed attack.

'It must have been 7 July when I was visiting my forward posts and looked down on Mametz Wood at a few hundred yards' range. I was by a Lewis gun post when I became aware of an attack in progress by what I believe were the 6th Dorsets [of 17th Division, then attacking Mametz Wood from the west while the Welsh division's 115th Brigade was attacking from the east]. They were creeping forward and using rifle grenades against the strip of wood jutting out towards us. I had never heard of this attack and got covering fire to work as quickly as possible, but the Lewis gun jammed and the attack fizzled out . . . . . We occupied a position from which very heavy covering fire could have been brought to bear had this been organised. '

During the action Private J Harris of the 6th Dorsets crawled out and went to the assistance of a badly wounded man of the 15th Royal Welsh Fusiliers. After dressing his wounds Private Harris under heavy fire brought him in although wounded five times himself.

At the end of operations on the night of 7/8 July XV Corps which Lieutenant-General Horne had intended to be in position to launch an assault on the main German second line had not gained a single yard of ground and in spite of all efforts of both the 17th and 38th Divisions had achieved nothing.

LIEUTENANT LIONEL DUNCAN STANBURY

He was born on 26 August 1885 to his parents Emma and John who lived in Worcester Park, Surrey. He attended Kings College School, Wimbledon, where he was active in the school's Officer Training Corps.

On the outbreak of war at nineteen years of age he joined the army on 16 September 1914 signing on at Westminster and immediately applied for a commission. He was small of stature, being only 5 feet 5½ inches tall and weighing only about 10 stone. The bespectacled young man with fair hair and blue eyes was soon accepted. He went to France in early February 1916.

Lieutenant Lionel Duncan Stanbury

He was considered to possess excellent leadership qualities and was specially commended for his efforts in leading the men who saved the machine gun crews on 6 July in Shelter Wood. The next day he himself was dead. According to one eye-witness he was hit in the left leg by a fragmenting shell and his leg was virtually severed below the knee. He was on the parapet of the German held Quadrangle Support Trench at the time and Sergeant J K Smith dragged him back about twenty five yards to a shell hole where a stretcher bearer of the 9th Duke of Wellingtons Regiment bandaged him up.

Second-Lieutenant J Michell crawled out with Sergeant Smith and another man to where Sergeant Smith indicated he had left Lieutenant Stanbury before concluding that his fellow officer had either been hit by another shell or buried in a shell hole.

The telegram arrived at his home on 13 July and then began a long wait for his distraught parents. His personal effects were returned, the inventory was as follows:

Correspondence
One pair puttees
One holdall
One air cushion in a case
One shirt
One towel
Razor blades

Statements were taken from all the men involved in the incident and Second-Lieutenant Michell was awarded the Military Cross. Over the proceeding months enquiries were made through the American Diplomatic Service in Germany for any news of Lieutenant Stanbury, in case he had been taken prisoner.

Every few months his case was reviewed and his file passed through the appropriate departments but always arrived back with a negative response. Finally late in March 1917 a decision was taken to officially presume him to be dead. The war office wrote to his father asking for confirmation that he himself had no other information.

On 24 March 1917 John Stanbury replied on writing paper edged in black.

> *In answer to yours of the 20th Inst. I beg to inform you that I have not received any information as to the fate of my Dear Boy, Lieutenant L. D. Stanbury.*
>
> *I have the honour to be*
> *your obedient servant*
> *J. Stanbury*

The official letter of condolence was sent on 3 April 1917. Under article 497 every bereaved relative received a payment. However Lieutenant Stanbury had received a month's pay in advance for July 1916. The final payment was reduced by amount not 'earned' during the period 8 - 31st of July 1916

Allowances	£79. 5. 10
less overpaid 8 - 31st July	10. 4. 0
	69. 1. 10

Chapter Five

INIQUITOUS FOLLY
8 July

Before dawn the three battalions who had unsuccessfully attacked the previous evening, the 10th Sherwood Foresters, the 7th East Yorks and the 6th Dorsets were relieved. Taking their place was the 7th Borders on the left and replacing the two battalions in the centre and on the right was the 7th Green Howards.

XV Corps issued orders for another bombing assault on Quadrangle Support Trench. This would be the fourth attempt and instead of a frontal assault over the open it was planned to attack along the trenches at each end. On the left the 7th Borders would attack from where it joined Pearl Alley and the 7th Green Howards attack from the right hand end by bombing up Quadrangle Alley. The idea was to meet up in the middle.

At 7.00am the attack was delivered. The 7th Borders pushed forward up Pearl Alley and bombed up as far as the Cemetery but could not reach the junction of that trench with Quadrangle Support Trench. The trenches were over the knees in mud and in places flooded up to the waist in water. The mud was very impeding and stuck like glue. Eventually they reached the junction but were then bombarded by German artillery. If that was not enough they then found themselves facing the German counter-attack from both sides. Once again the assault had been unsupported and the 7th Borders were fired on from Contalmaison on the left flank as well as Quadrangle Support on their right.

Similarly on the left the 7th Green Howards found mud up to four feet deep in Quadrangle Alley and could progress no further than 100 yards up the alley where the ground was swept by heavy machine fire from both sides, Attempts to break through continued for five hours until by 12.00 noon it was apparent no further progress could be expected.

In the afternoon the 17th Division were asked for the fifth time to attempt to capture Quadrangle Support Trench once again by bombing attacks. This was intended to coincide with an attack by the 23rd Division on the village of Contalmaison, which would have meant that the 7th Borders would not be exposed on their left flank. This information, however, proved erroneous as no such attack was planned. Nevertheless they were ordered to press on. The artillery bombardment

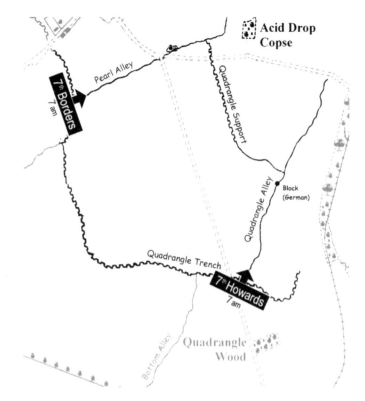

Map 11. The bombers' assault on Quadrangle Support Trench 8 July.

preceded the attack which commenced at 5.50pm. The 7th Borders and 7th Green Howards went forward again, reinforced by bombers of other battalions. First reports indicated that the 7th Borders had penetrated into Quadrangle Support Trench but news of progress was very slow in coming and very vague. The 7th Green Howards again failed to make progress past the strong point in Quadrangle Alley but on the right the 6th Dorsets attacking later at 8.50pm met with some success under the command of Major D Hughes-Onslow. A bombing squad led by Lance Corporal Routliffe assembled in the eastern end of Quadrangle Trench and rushing across the railway line in the valley got into the end of Wood Trench, following the route taken by Siegfried Sassoon. They bombed their way westwards up the trench and were able to establish a 'stop' within fifty yards of Mametz Wood. They were followed by a battle patrol led by Second-Lieutenant Moss and Private Hicks, who consolidated the trench some five hours before the appointed time and captured a large quantity of arms and ammunition. A trench of five feet in depth was then dug and connected Wood Trench with Quadrangle Trench. The whole operation had been co-ordinated by Captain O'Hanlon who subsequently held the trench against several German counter attacks. This advance had been planned as a preliminary attack to support and link with the 38th Division who were due to attack the southern end of Mametz Wood at 2.00am.

On the eastern side of the wood the 38th Division were struggling to reconcile the orders of XV Corps who had indicated that they required the attack on the previous evening of the 15th Royal Welsh Fusiliers on Strip Trench to be 'supported and developed'. The 38th Division asked for clarification. Up to that point all orders from XV Corps had been long, detailed and at times complex to the point, as we have seen of being confusing. Their reply marked a departure from that policy and their rather terse response was that the raid was to be made on something like a company front and that the 'place must be chosen by the commander of 113 Brigade now holding the line, who should carry out the raid and fix the exact point. Neither, Corps nor Division not being on the spot could fix this'. Accordingly orders were drawn up but it was proposed to attack with the whole battalion of the 14th Royal Welsh Fusiliers

A message was sent at 9.05pm from 38th Division to XV Corps which stated:

'113 BDE (15th Royal Welsh Fusiliers) made a bombing attack yesterday evening up Strip Trench but was driven back. The 113 BDE now preparing to make an attack up Strip Trench with one battalion. Hour of attack not yet settled.'

In reply at 10.35am Lieutenant-General Horne himself telephoned Major General Phillips and told him again he did not want a complete battalion attack by the 14th Royal Welsh Fusiliers which would be isolated at the southern end of the wood that and that he was on his way to see him at 38th Divisional Headquarters.

It is not difficult to judge Lieutenant-General Horne's demeanour as he made the journey from Heilly to see Major General Phillips at Grovetown and evidence of this can be drawn from the fact that the copy of the telephoned message sent to 38th Division which was to be kept in the file at XV Corps Headquarters was heavily endorsed in bold handwriting – possibly by Horne himself – 'Told to stop this attack' and 'Keep carefully.'

Whatever was said at the meeting between Horne and Phillips the end result was that the proposed attack on Strip Trench by the 38th Division was postponed and rescheduled to take place on the night of 8/9 July.

Later that afternoon XV Corps issued the orders as discussed between Horne and Phillips which the division fixed to take place at 2.00am on the 8 July. What occurred in the time between the order being issued to 38th Division Headquarters and the orders being received by the officer responsible for launching the attack is not clear. Lieutenant-Colonel G H Gwyther, commanding the 14th Royal Welsh Fusiliers was still unaware he was not to attack with his whole battalion and wrote later that he was very surprised to learn, only late in the evening of the 8 July, that the attack was not to be undertaken by a battalion but on a much smaller scale than he originally thought, by only one platoon and he had to reorganise at the last moment. Lieutenant Colonel Gwyther continues:

> 'The party started off down the communication trench leading to the front line and our starting place in good time under normal conditions; as however the communication trench was full of other troops of our brigade, progress was so slow that I attempted to get to the position overground, but found that our advance was so impeded by barbed wire and other obstacles that I considered it advisable to resort to the communication trench again, and the result was that the party arrived very late at the point from which the attack was to be made. Daylight was commencing, the element of surprise was problematical and I therefore decided not to risk men's lives unnecessarily and reported the situation to Brigade Headquarters.'

9 July

As dawn broke on Sunday 9 July a message was sent from 38th Divisional Headquarters to XV Corps which was received at 4.10am giving news of the failure of the 14th Royal Welsh Fusiliers to make their attack.

The performance of both the 38th Division and the 17th Division had already come under scrutiny and been questioned by Sir Douglas Haig himself and he had recorded in his diary that Lieutenant General Horne was enquiring into General Phillips' conduct as Divisional Commander. Under pressure from Haig and following his visit to see Phillips on the afternoon of 8 July, Horne was compelled to act. At 6.30am he ordered an investigation into why the attack failed.

It seems, though, whatever the investigation revealed, Phillips' fate was already decided. Ten minutes later the following order was sent to 38th Divisional Headquarters:

> '6.40am Corps Commander desires to see Major-General Phillips at Corps Headquarters at once.'

Thick tangled undergrowth of Mametz Wood. TAYLOR LIBRARY

It could not have been a comfortable journey to Heilly for Major-General Phillips, a man of some status and influence as a Member of Parliament and he may not have been well prepared to receive his dismissal and orders to return to England. The precise time of his departure is not recorded but it is likely that having had his orders to come 'at once' he had departed by the time Major-General A A Montgomery telephoned from Fourth Army Headquarters at 10.20am.

Major-General C G Blackader had already been summoned to XV Corps Headquarters to take over the 38th Division, but the Montgomery telephone call was to forestall that decision. Montgomery said that the Commander-in-Chief, Sir Douglas Haig had intervened and suggested that Major-General Watts, currently commanding the 7th Division, should take over the 38th Division and 'dispose of it as he wished.'

When Major-General Blackader arrived just fifteen minutes later he was told of the new arrangements and left to report to Fourth Army Headquarters. Major-General Watts arrived at 11.10am and was instructed to review the situation and make all arrangements to launch an attack in Mametz Wood which should be undertaken as soon as possible. Thus the flurry of activity and the arrivals and departures at Heilly mid-morning on the 9 July left Major-General Watts, as Haig's choice, with the initiative, while Lieutenant-General Horne's influence, for the time being at least, somewhat diminished.

If the news on the morning of the 9 July at XV Corps Headquarters from the 38th Division had been, to say the least, disappointing, it was little better from the 17th Division. Although Wood Trench had been taken and held by the 6th Dorsets news of the failure of the fifth and most recent attack on Quadrangle Support Trench was not received well. As well as having to deal with the leadership crisis of the 38th Division the pressure was increasing to show some results from the efforts of the 17th Division to clear the Quadrangle. XV Corps with growing impatience urged the 17th Division on and in a telephoned message at 8.20am which had a flavour of desperation, threw plenty of advice at Major-General Pilcher but, strangely, there followed no detailed orders for an attack or an alternative idea on how to capture Quadrangle Support Trench. Pilcher was urged to use fresh troops to attack Quadrangle Support today, but the message continued 'the plan must be yours ... at an hour to be fixed by yourself ... and get in the best way you can.'

Pilcher, we know, had been critical of some of the orders he had received and had not been slow to voice these criticisms and it is possible that Lieutenant-General Horne decided to concede and give Pilcher the opportunity to prove his point. We also know that General Rawlinson was impatient and was never convinced that the capture of Mametz Wood was a necessary precursor to the main assault planned on the Bazentin-Longueval front and he was drawing support from his commanders – including Horne – to convince Sir Douglas Haig of the validity of his plans. With Major-General Watts in firm control of the 38th Division, Horne, therefore, by also giving Major-General Pilcher some autonomy would neatly give himself some

Lieutenant-General Henry Horne Commander of XV Corps.

respite and find time to attend to the demands of General Rawlinson.

In another departure, XV Corps belatedly conceded that an unsupported attack by the 17th Division, a point argued by Major-General Pilcher, should be avoided if possible. Referring to a proposed attack by 23rd Division on Contalmaison on the left, Horne said he now thought the better battle plan would be to wait until that had been achieved but in a clear criticism of the way the battalions of the 17th Division had been deployed urged that, whatever, fresh troops should be used and said that 'it is no use attacking two or three times with the same troops.' In another concession the decision on the artillery bombardments were to be left to the discretion of the 17th Division. By now, instead of being the forerunner to a joint attack on Mametz Wood with the 38th Division, the capture of Quadrangle Support Trench in front of Pilchers' troops had become a major objective itself.

The 7th Green Howards it will be recalled, had already made two unsuccessful attacks up Quadrangle Alley to break through the 'block' and capture the junction of the Alley and Quadrangle Support Trench. They were ordered again to make their third attempt, and the sixth overall to break through. The attack was timed to commence at 3.35 am on 9 July and was in isolation, no other attack being attempted from the right flank in Pearl Alley. 50 Brigade and 17th Divisional diaries both omit to record much detail of the attack except that it failed. The 7th Green Howards diary fails to make any reference at all.

On the extreme right the valiant efforts of the 7th Borders who had been subjected to heavy fire from both sides at the western end of Quadrangle Trench and up Pearl Alley were concluded when they were relieved by the 7th Lincolns. They too were ordered to hold on at all costs. During the morning of 9 July orders were received from Major-General Pilcher by the 7th Lincolns and the 7th Green Howards to make the seventh attack on Quadrangle Support.

It will be recalled that Pilcher had been told that he should co-operate with the 23rd Division, and avoid an isolated attack. He was also told that the attack on Contalmaison was to take place at midday. Accordingly, Pilcher timed his advance for 12.15pm. Preparations were made and additional Stokes mortar emplacements were constructed in Quadrangle Trench. The 7th Green Howards on the right in Quadrangle Alley were withdrawn and the 'block' in the Alley which had so far denied all attempts to cross it was bombarded with 6″ Howitzers in an attempt to break it up, prior to the assault. There was an artillery bombardment of one hour and fifteen minutes prior to the advance and once again the 7th Green Howards set off up Quadrangle

Prefix.......... Code...,..........m.	Words	Charge	This message is on a/c of :	Recd. at...................m.
Office of Origin a service Instructions.				
	Sent		.....................Service.	Date....................
SECRET	At................... m.			From...................
S.D.R.	To			
	By.		(Signature of "Franking Officer.")	By....................

TO {   17th Division   6|A|11

Sender's Number	Day of Month	In reply to Number	
G 874.	9		A A A

    The enclosed air report of last evening's attack is forwarded for information.

    The Corps Commander holds that this report bears out his opinion that QUADRANGLE SUPPORT has not been strongly held for some time past.

    He is of opinion that the want of success is due to the fatigue of the troops on the spot and is convinced that a determined and well organised attack by fresh troops should make certain of the capture of this trench.

    He directs me to impress upon you the great importance of making a success of the attack which you are now preparing in accordance with my telephone message of 8.20 a.m. this morning.

From	15th Corps		
Place			
Time	10.20 a.m.		Br. Genl.

The above may be forwarded as now corrected.   (Z)   G.S.

            Censor.   Signature of Addressor or person authorised to telegraph in his name.

Alley towards the 'block'.

The Stokes mortar guns in Quadrangle Alley were unable to fire at all because of the soft and muddy ground which made them unstable. The 7th Green Howards found the mud very heavy and any attempt to make a rapid advance was impossible and quickly exhausted the men who were once more under fire from machine guns. The German machine gun positions noted from the previous attack had been subjected to bombardment and counter-fire from the British machine

Germans under bombardment.

guns, but with plenty of options, especially on the right in Mametz
Wood, the German crews simply moved to an alternative site and
carried out their effective work. Any troops advancing slowly up the
relatively shallow and badly damaged Quadrangle Alley trench were
easy targets.

On the right flank, similarly, no progress was made by the 7th
Lincolns who attempted to move up Pearl Alley and capture the
junction of the Alley and Quadrangle Support Trench.

At 1.00pm one company of the 8th South Staffordshires was called
up to reinforce the 7th Lincolns in Quadrangle Trench. With progress
over the open in daylight impossible in the face of machine gun fire
and progress through the trenches prevented by mud and strong points
the seventh attempt to capture Quadrangle Support Trench was
abandoned.

(2679) Wt. W.6065-2652. 35m lifts. 7.15. F.T. & Co., Ltd. Forms G 2120 / 4

Army Form C. 2120.

6/A/22

ARMY TELEPHONE MESSAGE.

Date 9/7.	Time handed in 3.15 p.m.	Time { Sent:— .... m. Received:— .... m.

To 17th Divn.

Situation has been explained to 23rd Div. and they will make their attack separately. QUADRANGLE SUPPORT trench to be taken tonight by 17th Div. You can make a surprise attack without any warning at at all by using the Flammenwerfer as it goes. That will surprise enemy more than anything. Machine guns will not stop fresh troops if they mean to get in. Understand you have fresh troops in front and not those who have been engaged all night. Impress upon troops that they are going to be relieved tomorrow night, that it is their last show, and it is up to them to make their reputation by taking the trench before they go. Your attack is not contingent on that of the 23rd in any way. Whether they attack or not: whether they succeed or not, 17th Div. are to have the trench.

From:— XV Corps

Name of ~~receiver~~ sender

Brig.
G.S

Major-General Pilcher could hardly have failed to notice that the promised assault on Contalmaison by the 23rd Division he had prepared his attack to coincide with had failed to take place and once again an isolated and piecemeal assault had ended in failure.

While all this was taking place, XV Corps despatched a message at 11.10am that stated that during the morning air reconnaissance was made of the 17th Divisional front. Lieutenant-General Horne expressed his opinion as to the reason for the want of success of the attacks of the previous night again taking the opportunity to criticise the deployment of the troops of the 17th Division.

At 2.00pm another message was sent to both 38th Division and the 17th Division stating that prisoners captured within the last twenty four hours had given information about German withdrawal and they had said that there would be little opposition to a concentrated attack in strength. The prisoners had said they were surprised that the British attacked in such small numbers 'in twos and threes' and XV Corps again urged the utmost determination and vigour.

These comments seem to overlook several things. Firstly, proposals to put in heavier attacks, especially by the 38th Division on the 7 July and also the failed attack on the night of 8/9 July had been overturned by XV Corps. Secondly, Major-General Pilcher's opinion that the effect of machine guns and the likely failure of unsupported attacks on the Quadrangle were disregarded. The casualties were mounting and the ranks were thinning with some battalions of the 17th Division at less than half strength. The exceptionally heavy concentration of machine gun fire facing the attackers was reducing the numbers to such an extent that by the time the German positions were reached it would probably appear to the German defenders that the assault was made with only small numbers. Another factor to remember is that, even assuming the withdrawal they refer to took place prior to the night of 6 July this message was sent at 2.00pm on the 9 July and the information was somewhat out of date. Indeed, German reports later proved that encouraged by the ease with which they repulsed the attack of the 38th Division on the morning of 7 July the Germans had decided to reinforce Mametz Wood and the Quadrangle.

At 3.15pm yet another sternly worded message from XV Corps made no apology for the confusion over the intentions of the 23rd Division, which had intended no such action at all, but took the opportunity to emphasise Lieutenant-General Horne's belief that the troops of the 17th Division had not been efficiently deployed and had not been determined enough in the face of the German machine guns.

Signallers in the cellars of Fricourt Chateau.

During the afternoon a conference was held at Fricourt Chateau with officers of 50 and 51 Brigades and staff of the 17th Division Headquarters to plan the capture of Quadrangle Support Trench.

Similarly at Grovetown some five miles away Major-General Watts at 38th Divisional Head-quarters was engaged in preparing a battle plan that would finally ensure the capture of Mametz Wood. Watts decided to throw the greater weight of the 38th Division against Mametz Wood, but this time the attack was to be on the southern portion of the Wood. Sir Douglas Haig was still insistent on the Wood being in British hands before the planned main assault and during the same afternoon had travelled to Heilly and visited Lieutenant-General Horne. Horne, under such direct pressure sent a message to the 38th Division saying that the 'Commander-in-Chief had visited the Corps Commander and impressed upon him the great importance of the occupation of Mametz Wood.

10 July

The first attack to take place on the night of 9/10 July was to be launched by the 17th Division at 11.20pm. No consideration appears to have been given co-ordinating the efforts of the two divisions and the attack of the 38th Division was timed to commence at 4.00am. Dealing first then, with the 17th Division, at the suggestion of XV Corps Major-General Pilcher devised a surprise night frontal attack, over the open with the intention of taking Quadrangle Support Trench by the bayonet.

As a preliminary to the assault orders were given to the 7th Lincolns to attack Pearl Alley initially and capture the junction of Pearl Alley and Quadrangle Support Trench and so safeguard the left flank of the 8th South Staffordshires who were to make the main attack.

The main attack was to be delivered over the open on the front of Quadrangle Support Trench. The 8th South Staffordshires would take the major part of the trench (350 yards) on the left while the 7th Green Howards would capture the block in Quadrangle Alley and 50 yards of Quadrangle Support on the right. The portion of the trench left between these two points was then to be cleared during the remainder of the night.

Before looking at what happened during the attack it is interesting to see how the Germans had been able hold out particularly in Quadrangle Support Trench against repeated artillery bombardment, bombing and infantry attacks.

The reports that the trench was lightly held may well have been accurate but as we have seen it was situated in open country sandwiched between Contalmaison and Mametz Wood from which heavy machine gun fire from both positions could be directed across its front. At each flank a communication trench connected it to the rear (Pearl Alley and Quadrangle Alley) and these had also originally provided access forward to Quadrangle Trench. It was therefore possible to re-inforce Quadrangle Support at either end as long as the two junctions held out and with a frontal attack as the British discovered, an impossibility even by night because of enfilading machine gun fire from both flanks, the trench could be held by concentrating on the defence of the junctions.

The trench was held by the 11th Company of the 122nd Reserve Infantry Regiment commanded by Lieutenant Irion. He had constructed a large 'block' near the junction of the trench with Pearl Alley with sandbags and it was protected by a machine gun. As a communication trench Pearl Alley was fairly straight and provided limited cover and protection for any troops advancing up it. On the other flank as we know a 'block' some twenty yards from the junction with Quadrangle Support had provided very adequate protection for the German troops defending the junction. On the higher ground

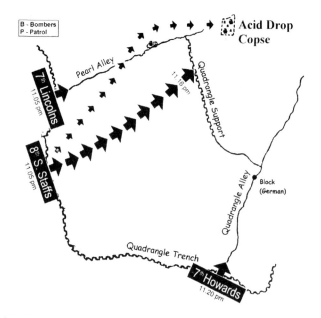

Map 12. The Bayonet attack on Quadrangle Support Trench 10 July.

behind the trench, machine guns were able to provide additional frontal fire over the top of the trench from Acid Drop Copse.

At 4.50pm the battalion bombers of the 7th Lincolns led the preliminary attack supported by one company of infantry with orders to clear Pearl Alley. The 7th Lincolns again found the going equally as hard. In Pearl Alley the mud was just as deep and clinging and inhibited every attempt to get forward. Lieutenant Jones who led the assault with the bombers sent a message back at 7.45pm reporting that because of the conditions it was even impossible to stand securely to throw grenades with any effect, at all, and the battalion returned to Quadrangle Trench.

Lieutenant-Colonel W A J Barker commanding the 8th South Staffordshires had made meticulous preparations during the evening for the main assault. He reconnoitred the ground with his company commanders and detailed B and D Companies to lead the attack in three waves. A Company was to be in reserve and C to remain in Quadrangle Trench. Orders were issued for complete silence and all accessories to equipment removed. Bayonets were to be covered in mud in case the moon glinted on them. Battalion bombers were not only to accompany the infantry but also detailed to assist the 7th Lincolns in Pearl Alley where they had previously made no headway. Wire cutters were issued in case the wire was substantially intact in front of the German trench. New telephone wires were run up from Battalion Headquarters to Quadrangle Trench. As darkness fell white tapes were laid out in the open in front of Quadrangle Support Trench to enable the troops to line up and attack in the right direction.

At 10.45pm an officer patrol went forward to locate any enemy listening posts and all was ready by 11.00pm. At 11.05pm the eighth attempt began under undirected but sweeping machine gun fire from the direction of Contalmaison. The attacking companies made quick progress and were already in the enemy trench before the agreed start time. This, however, left the 7th Green Howards on the right with the disadvantage of facing an enemy already alerted and waiting for them. Already depleted, only one company of forty men led by Captain Barmby attacked across the open four minutes later but were met with intense fire and no-one got into the trench.

Attacking in greater numbers the 8th South Staffordshires had entered Quadrangle Support Trench in the face of machine gun fire, rifle fire and bombs. In hand to hand combat a section of the trench

German machine gun crew operating over a trench 'block' of sandbags in a smashed and flooded trench.

was cleared. The 7th Lincolns made no progress up Pearl Alley but the battalion bombers of the 8th South Staffordshires left the trench and advanced over the open as far as Acid Drop Copse, albeit with heavy losses.

In Quadrangle Support the outnumbered Germans led by Lieutenant Irion were all but overwhelmed, they were pushed back to the western end of the trench from where the 7th Green Howards had been repelled. Lieutenant Irion managed to form another 'block' with sandbags and protected it with a machine gun and so prevented total capture of the position. The attack progressed as far as Acid Drop Copse where the 8th South Staffordshires set up a machine gun post. On the British right the 7th Green Howards again approached the 'block' in Quadrangle Alley defended by the German 10th and 12th Companies.

At 12.35am Lieutenant Brooke of the 7th Green Howards managed to get back to Quadrangle Trench where the 7th East Yorks were waiting in support. He reported the attack had failed again and that Captain Barmby had been severely wounded. The original orders of the 7th East Yorks had been to move forward and hold the block and junction in Quadrangle Alley after the 7th Green Howards had captured it. However they were ordered forward immediately as re-inforcements and forty men led by Second-Lieutenant Goodwin took up more bombs. By 2.30am a third attack had not yet been organised and reports were coming through that the assault on the left by the 8th South Staffordshires had failed. 50 Brigade Headquarters ordered a withdrawal before daylight. On hearing this Major-General Pilcher immediately countermanded it, ordering the attack to be pushed home. This was received at 50 Brigade Headquarters at 3.08am and this was sent on at once. However the order to withdraw had already reached the front line and the troops were on their way back. Finding the trenches blocked with troops, wounded and equipment they returned over the open and so missed Pilcher's order as it was sent forward by runner. As it happened 17th Division just half an hour later called the whole attack off at 3.40am and thus the mix up eventually saved the 7th Green Howards who were being regrouped at the time to make the attack.

Lieutenant-Colonel Barker was desperately looking for support from either flank and while holding on was taking heavy casualties. Machine guns from the direction of Contalmaison were playing heavily on the rear of Quadrangle Support, and not troubled by further attacks from the right Lieutenant Irion in the western end of the trench re-organised and led a heavy counter attack with his bombers against the 8th South Staffordshires occupying the other part of the trench. The assault was held off but by now the Pioneer Company should have arrived to build strong points and reinforce the trench. They had got lost on the way forward and Lieutenant-Colonel Barker sent six different runners to find them. They eventually arrived at 2.30am but by 2.45am Lieutenant-Colonel Barker, aware that his men were now being pushed back down Pearl Alley felt he could hold on no longer without support from either the right or left and would be left further exposed in the approaching daylight. Instructions were given at 3.30am to withdraw to Quadrangle Trench bringing all wounded men back and this was successfully achieved. The exception to this was a patrol occupying Acid Drop Copse where they had set up a machine gun post. News of the withdrawal never reached them and they remained isolated in enemy territory. Lieutenant Irion was eventually able to re-occupy the major part of Quadrangle Support Trench unopposed and the casualties of the 8th South Staffordshires were nineteen officers and over 200 other ranks.

Lieutenant Irion's troops in Quadrangle Support were badly in need of reinforcement and assistance was to be soon arriving. On the evening of 9 July behind the German second line in Martinpuich the 6th Company of the 122nd Reserve Infantry Regiment under its commanding officer Lieutenant Köstlin was preparing to comply with orders to move towards Mametz Wood. His men had to re-stock with ammunition and grenades and were about to have a meal from the battalion field kitchen cart before setting out on their journey. Just then

British troops making their way through shattered trees. TAYLOR LIBRARY

a British shell landed and the horse pulling the cart bolted in terror taking the cart, food and everything else away into the darkness!

It was after midnight when the company finally left Martinpuich loaded with ammunition and two machine guns. Guides from the 3rd Battalion were supposed to lead the way through the trenches but Lieutenant Köstlin decided to push on across the open, marching on a compass bearing. The journey between Martinpuich and Bazentin was very slow and the men soon became very spread out with great difficulty being encountered crossing the shell holes and trenches. As they moved across the German second line at Bazentin the British shelling got heavier, shrapnel shells sometimes burst causing casualties among his men. Nearing Mametz Wood he decided not to enter it as it would be very easy to get lost and made for the open country between the wood and Contalmaison. It was his intention to reach the wood by going down Pearl Alley and along Quadrangle Support.

After crossing the Bazentin-Contalmaison road the company halted and the guides went forward to see where they were required. About twenty minutes the guides came back and told Lieutenant Köstlin to move straight ahead where reinforcements were urgently needed. it was now approaching 3.00am and they had not gone much further when a machine gun suddenly opened up at short range on higher ground on their right.

The gun crew of the 8th South Staffordshires in Acid Drop Copse were unable to take very accurate aim at the German columns as there was only just a glimmer of daylight but the Germans scattered. Attempting to rally his men Lieutenant Köstlin urged them to dash forward to the cover of their trench. It was further than he thought , over 300 yards and only thirty of his men eventually made it safely. Some were casualties, some hid in shell holes while others ran back towards the German main position near Bazentin.

Lieutenant Köstlin joined up with Lieutenant Irion in Quadrangle Support Trench where all communication with Battalion Headquarters in Mametz Wood had been lost since midnight. His last orders were to act independently without waiting for battalion instructions. As the senior officer present, Lieutenant Köstlin then took over command of the trench. The total strength holding it, including the new arrivals was six officers and 160 other ranks.

Chapter Six

THEY WENT WITH SONGS TO BATTLE
10 July

Mametz Wood was the first and largest of those woods that the British and Dominion troops were to capture during the Battle of the Somme. The Wood was intersected by rides or avenues but these had been blocked in many places. During the previous two years it had grown wild through neglect and in parts the undergrowth was very dense. Shelling had damaged many of the tall trees which had splintered and fallen, causing additional hazards to the barbed wire - erected by the Germans.

The 38th Division attack plan differed only from that being prepared by Major-General Phillips prior to his departure in that it was to be a heavier attack with an initial assault of four battalions. The main innovation was an elaborate artillery bombardment Two different methods were to be used, the first was to proceed with a conventional bombardment on the German front line and lift back when the expected attack would normally be delivered. The defending troops would emerge from their dugouts to meet their attackers. The artillery, though, would then drop back on to the front line and find the exposed defenders. The second was to use a creeping barrage through the Wood. The idea of this kind of barrage was to place a protective curtain of shells just in front of the advancing infantry which would be timed to lift back at regular intervals to allow the advance to proceed. All this, of course, depended on good artillery observation and very accurate work by the gunners. The creeping barrage was organised to commence at 4.15am and lift forward fifty yards every minute to just beyond the first objective which would give the infantry two hours to reach and consolidate their position. At 6.15am it would move on again to the second objective and again one hour later at 7.15am it would lift to the northern edge of the Wood.

During the early hours of 10 July the attacking battalions assembled in their positions forward of White Trench on Fusilier Ridge overlooking the rising ground over which they were to make the attack. The disposition of the assaulting troops placed the 16th Royal Welsh Fusiliers on the extreme left of the attack. Overlooking Strip Trench, they had the shortest distance to travel to reach the edge of the Wood. Following behind them would be the 14th Royal Welsh Fusiliers. In the centre of the attack from their forward position the 14th Welsh

Regiment had about 500 yards to travel and on the extreme right the 13th Welsh Regiment had an advance of up to 750 yards.

The 38th Division orders made brief reference to the 17th Division and mentioned co-operation on the eastern side of the Wood where the 6th Dorsets were still holding Wood Trench and also to attacks on Quadrangle Support Trench, but no specific instructions were issued except that in the attack on Strip Trench care should be taken in remembering the 6th Dorsets position, especially by the trench mortar batteries in Cliff Trench and Queen's Nullah.

Lying in wait for the Welshmen in the southern part of the wood were the 2nd Battalion of the Lehr Infantry Regiment which was part of the 3rd Guards Division. The Lehr Regiment were highly professional soldiers and had been specially selected before the war to train drafts of the Prussian Army. Later the Kaiser's personal body guard was created with elements drawn from the Regiment.

The attacking battalions were in position by 3.00am on the morning of the attack which at that time was cool but dry. The day was to become very hot and humid with thick cloud and temperatures in the lower eighties. Both attacking brigades were to be supported by machine gun crews. Initially eight guns were to be taken in by the 113th Brigade Machine Gun Company with the attack of the 16th Royal Welsh Fusiliers. Four of these would be in position along the road below Fusilier Ridge to cover the start of the advance. The other guns would go in with the third wave and consolidate the edge of the

Map 13. 38th Welsh Divisions' second attack on Mametz Wood 10 July.

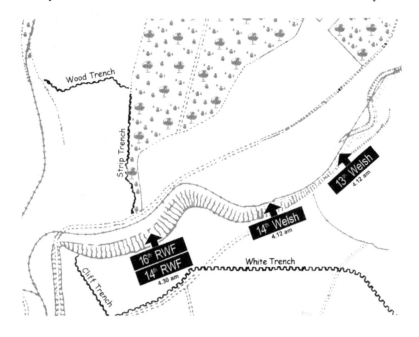

Aerial view of ground over which the attack of 10 July was delivered. Strip Trench points like a finger towards the left flank of the Welsh positions. The edge of 'Hammerhead' is on the extreme right. Caterpillar Wood in the foreground. (See Map 13)

wood. Similarly the 114th Brigade Machine Gun Company, commanded by Captain Job, were to take eight guns in with the 13th and 14th Welsh. Four were detailed to cover the centre of the wood while four were to cover the eastern edge of the wood. Additional guns were situated in Marlborough Copse and Caterpillar Wood to cover any counter attack on the eastern edge of the wood and the ground to the south. The artillery barrage opened up and lasted for forty five minutes and smoke barrages were put down along the whole of the front of the attack.

Overlooking Strip Trench, the 16th Royal Welsh Fusiliers, led by Lieutenant-Colonel Carden, held what amounted to a short religious service. They sang hymns in Welsh and their commanding officer addressed them. He said 'Boys make your peace with God! We are going to take that position and some us won't come back, But we are going to take it.'

As the first streaks of light brought the dawn the 13th and 14th Welsh moved forward before the appointed time because of the greater distance they had to travel. This caused some confusion for the 16th Royal Welsh Fusiliers as Carden who shortly before 4.00am had gone over to speak with officers of the other attacking battalions had not returned.

The soldier's view across the rising ground of the attack of 10 July.

Major McLellan who was second in command waited for Carden to return but by 4.12am when the battalion should have moved off there was no sign of him. McLellan tried to find the commanding officer but without success and by 4.30am assuming he had become a casualty gave the order to advance. As they reached the top of the ridge they saw some men already retiring and while a few men continued forward the majority of the 16th Royal Welsh Fusiliers also retired. At that point Lieutenant-Colonel Carden returned - the men were reorganised and the advance commenced again. Being late they lost the cover of the artillery barrage and as they advanced they were hit by fire not only from the front of the wood but also from Strip Trench and other German positions in the Quadrangle trench system.

Leading his men forward Carden tied a coloured handkerchief to his walking stick which he held up to give them a focal point on which to rally shouting "this will show you where I am". He was also a conspicuous figure to the Germans and he fell wounded. Refusing to give up he got up, struggled on and was again hit and this time fell dead at the edge of the wood.

Following the 16th Royal Welsh Fusiliers the 14th Royal Welsh Fusiliers attacked but with only two companies, the other two being left behind owing to a mistake in brigade orders. They too made initial progress towards the wood but also came under heavy fire about 200 yards from the wood.

Some men came running back shouting retire and there was much confusion. Major Mills and Captain Glynn-Jones attempted to regroup the men even threatening use of their revolvers to exercise control. Through all this there was heavy machine gun fire and artillery bombardment. Major Mills was killed and Glynn-Jones reorganised the men in the shelter of the railway embankment, below the ridge. Lieutenant-Colonel Gwyther, commanding the battalion, had been severely wounded but Glynn-Jones found him and organised evacuation. There seemed to be no British troops in front and no support from the rear and being isolated Glynn-Jones set up machine gun posts on each flank whilst sending two runners back to battalion headquarters asking for support. Meanwhile men were crawling back from shell holes in front with reports of heavy casualties, many among the officers and non-commissioned officers.

Lieutenant-Colonel
Ronald James Walter
Carden commanding 16th
Battalion RWF

In the centre the 14th Welsh were commanded by Lieutenant-Colonel J H Hayes and the battalion moved in good formation making quick progress under the leadership of Captain Godfrey leading B Company and Captain Dagge leading C company. Casualties were slight until the edge of the wood was reached as the enemy had been unprepared for the attacking troops to be so close to the barrage. Captain Wilson distinguished himself at the head of his company by bayoneting a burly German and then with a single shot brought down a sniper who was hiding in a tree. Lieutenant Hawkins equally brave charged and captured two machine guns on separate occasions although he was wounded the second time. The battalion took casualties in the latter stages of the advance with the second in command Major Brock Williams being wounded and three company commanders were also casualties.

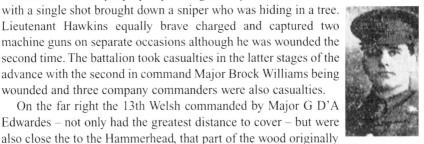

Lieutenant F
J Hawkins a
Welsh Rugby
Union
International

On the far right the 13th Welsh commanded by Major G D'A Edwardes – not only had the greatest distance to cover – but were also close the to the Hammerhead, that part of the wood originally attacked on 7 July. The Germans had machine gun positions in that part of the Hammerhead immediately to the right of the assaulting troops and they were able to enfilade the attack with heavy fire. Although the 13th Welsh had moved 150 yards to the left on the approach to the wood to foreshorten the distance to be covered and to ensure contact was made with the 14th Welsh in the centre, casualties were heavy and those arriving at the edge of the wood also met with heavy resistance. An attempt to enter the wood was repulsed. Reinforcements came forward and a second attempt was also thrown back. A third attempt was made and this time the 13th Welsh managed to get into the wood and some prisoners were taken. Once in the wood they found the undergrowth very dense and the only clear passages were through where the artillery shells had struck whilst cleverly placed machine gun positions swept the obvious approaches.

At 4.30am the 10th Welsh were drawn into the battle and sent one company forward to assist. They were soon followed by the remainder of the battalion. They suffered heavily from machine gun fire from the direction of the Hammerhead and the portion of the wood nearby that had not been attacked because the 13th Welsh had veered to the left. Lieutenant-Colonel P E Ricketts the commanding officer was twice wounded going down the slope, from the ridge. One bullet cut the femoral artery but he refused to be taken away and continued for some time to direct the attack although he could only do so lying down and was unable to see clearly what was happening.

A platoon of A Company led by Second-Lieutenant Cowie advanced on the right towards the Hammerhead where they gained a foothold, silencing a machine gun and taking several prisoners. Second-Lieutenant Cowie was killed during the attack. Lieutenant Edwardes, too, captured two machine guns on separate occasions before being wounded. The remainder of the battalion entered the wood where it met up with elements of the 13th and 14th Welsh. The units in the wood were very mixed up and the situation was not helped by the British artillery barrage which was falling short. This was mainly due to their low trajectory causing shells to detonate on impact with the trees.

Meanwhile on the extreme left the 16th Royal Welsh Fusiliers had appealed for support having seen nothing of the 14th Royal Welsh Fusiliers led by Captain Glynn-Jones. All communications with 113th Brigade Headquarters had been cut so the 15th Royal Welsh Fusiliers moved to the attack before any orders had been given by brigade, but they too saw nothing of the 14th Battalion. Strip Trench was successfully bombed though heavy casualties were taken including the bombing officer of the 16th Royal Welsh Fusiliers, Second-Lieutenant Rees who was killed but both battalions made progress through the wood and the 15th Royal Welsh Fusiliers made contact with the 6th Dorsets in Wood Trench. Following close behind the 15th Royal Welsh Fusiliers two companies of the 13th Royal Welsh Fusiliers were moved from Danzig Alley to the Queen's Nullah and later entered the wood.

Thus, all four battalions of 113 Brigade were now committed to the attack.

The 14th Royal Welsh Fusiliers were still sheltering by the railway line and they saw the reinforcements of the 15th Royal Welsh Fusiliers enter Strip Trench. At about the same time some Germans came out of the wood with their hands up and a white flag was shown near the entrance to the main ride. They thought it might be a trick but allowed them to approach and then went forward to meet them. Glynn-Jones then sent a patrol forward to the wood. The rest of the battalion entered it at the entrance to the central ride running northwards and pushed ahead.

With representatives of seven battalions in the wood it was very congested. The troops however formed themselves into patrols and set about clearing the wood advancing quickly beyond the first objective. Units of the 13th and 14th Welsh outran the British barrage and at 4.50am Colonel Hayes commanding the 14th Welsh sent a message asking for the guns to lift. Another message was sent by Major Bond with the 13th Welsh at 5.10am stating that they were 'through the wood'. Colonel Hayes request was refused and all units were ordered to fall back. Many casualties occurred, due to British shell fire, including Major Bond who was killed. Major Edwardes was also killed and command passed to Captain Johnson who had only eight other

German gun abandoned in Mametz wood. The breech block has been removed so as to render it useless to the British. TAYLOR LIBRARY

Left: Bevan Brothers 14th Welsh.

Above left: Charles Mew 14th Welsh wounded in Mametz Wood, 10 July 1916.

Above right: D Davies, 13th Welsh killed 10 July, age 30, no known grave.

Top: Looking towards the hollow where under shelter of the railway embankment, Captain Glynn Jones reorganised the 14th Royal Welsh Fusiliers and attended to the wounded.

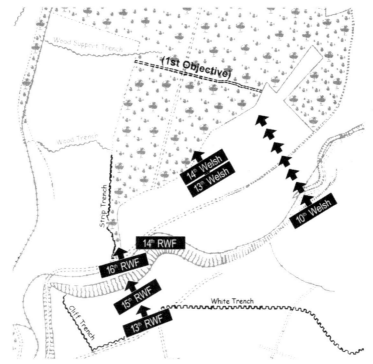

Map 14. The position at 4.30am – 5.00am 10 July.

officers left in his battalion. Later this was reduced to seven when Second-Lieutenant Purdie and Second-Lieutenant Crossman went out on patrol in the wood and Second-Lieutenant Crossman returned to give the news that Second-Lieutenant Purdie was dead.

Having been refused permission to press on Colonel Hayes began the task of organising the mass of troops at the first objective. Five commanders of the seven battalions involved had been killed or seriously wounded. He had help from Lieutenant-Colonel Bell the only other surviving battalion commander who instructed Captain Glynn-Jones to dig in to the rear of the line of the first objective on the right flank of the 6th Dorsets in Wood Trench.

The units of the three Royal Welsh Fusiliers battalions were concentrated on the western side of the wood facing Wood Support Trench on their left flank. In the centre the ground was held by the 14th Welsh and the right flank nearest the Hammerhead was held by the 10th and 13th Welsh – where German machine gunners still held out. The wait to advance was a nervous one. In addition to the German barrage snipers and machine guns were active from both flanks. When it came at 6.15am the British artillery barrage opened up and the troops moved forward. On the left the battalions of the Royal Welsh Fusiliers were attacked from Wood Support Trench and Quadrangle Alley.

Private David Jones 15th Royal Welsh Fusiliers author of *In Parenthesis*

Major d'Arcy Edwardes, Dragoon Guards attached Welsh Regiment killed in Mametz Wood.

Progress was very slow and disorganised and it was extremely difficult to find directions among the thick undergrowth and fallen trees. It was sometimes impossible to see more than a few yards forward and becoming totally disorientated some troops fired in the wrong direction on their own men at the slightest movement.

Private David Jones who was in the 15th Royal Welsh Fusiliers was another participant in the battle who, like Captain Wyn Griffith was to become a writer of some distinction after the war. His book *In Parenthesis* tells of his experiences in the war, the last part of his ordeal in Mametz Wood.

He was part of the congestion in the wood and describes the confusion thus:

'But which is front, which way's the way on and where's the corporal and what's this crush and all this shoving you along, and someone shouting rhetorically about remembering your nationality – and Jesus Christ – they're coming through the floor, endthwart and overlong:

Jerry's through on the flank ... and: Beat it! – that's what that one said as he ran past:

Bosches back in Strip Trench – its a monumental bollocks every time and but we avoid wisely there is but death'

Many confusing and conflicting reports had been received by Brigadier-General L A E Price-Davies at 113 Brigade Headquarters. Telephone wires had been cut and many runners were casualties from the German counter barrage. Messages that got through asked for reinforcements and Lieutenant-Colonel O S Flower commanding the 13th Royal Welsh Fusiliers was sent forward with the remaining two companies of the battalion. Price-Davies also sent staff officers for news, but with little result. He decided to go himself and set off

Major C E Bond, 13th Welsh Regiment came out of retirement and was gazetted in June 1915. KiA.

Sergeant T J Price 13th Welsh , wounded and lay out in the open for 36 hours before being found alive.

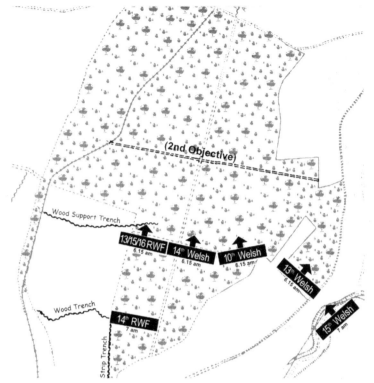

Map 15. The position at 6.15am 10 July.

with another officer. While making his way up Strip Trench he encountered a group of men, he was later to describe as 'running back in panic' and the troops in very unsteady condition with very few officers. The reinforcements of the 13th Royal Welsh Fusiliers also became mixed up in the concentration of troops at the first objective.

Over on the extreme right the 13th Welsh were attempting to push forward and consolidate the Hammerhead. They sent a message to 114 Brigade Headquarters in Pommiers Redoubt asking for reinforcements. Brigadier-General T O Marden commanding the brigade sent in the 15th Welsh under the command of Major P Anthony at about 7.00am. During the advance they were met by machine gun fire but managed to get through the enemy barrage as well with few casualties. Once in the wood they pushed on meeting little opposition except for a sniper and about twenty five Germans. By 7.45am they had established themselves on the eastern edge of the Hammerhead and sent two platoons of B company to establish contact with the 13th Welsh. At

Major P Anthony fought in South Africa,Queen's Medal with five Clasps. His family published the *Hereford Times.*

101

8.05am when contact had still not been made, a further platoon from A
Company was sent forward. Almost immediately it was noticed that the
Germans were massing in the road below Flat Iron Copse for a counter
attack. In addition to this a patrol of Germans with a machine gun had
entered the northern edge of the Hammerhead, got through the gap
between the battalion and the 10th Welsh, before the platoon from A
Company had arrived and got in behind the platoons of B Company
who were annihilated. Only four men eventually returned. The
battalion were also enfiladed by fire on the right flank from the
Germans now in the road along the eastern edge of the Hammerhead.
Major Anthony was killed by a sniper and the 15th Welsh had to fall
back in stages to the southern edge of the Hammerhead and dig in. Two
platoons of men from C and D Companies bravely, under the command
of Lieutenant J Evans, held on in the Hammerhead under intense
pressure and were the last to retire. Further casualties were taken from
machine gun and sniper fire including four more officers. The
Germans continued to attack the eastern edge of the wood from the
road where the British machine guns situated in Marlborough Copse
and Caterpillar Wood were unable to direct fire on them. Contact was
finally made with the 13th Welsh on the left at 9.30am.

Map 16. German patrol 8.00am 10 July.

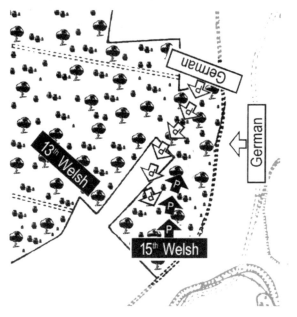

102

The road where the Germans massed to counter attack the eastern edge of the 'Hammerhead'. Flat Iron Copse Cemetery in the distance.

17th Division Support

On the western edge of the wood after the failure of the bayonet attack at night the 17th Division were instructed to co-operate with the attack on Mametz Wood. Further attacks on Quadrangle Alley and Quadrangle Support were to be made and patrols pushed forward to occupy the western edge of Mametz Wood. Major King prepared to attack Quadrangle Alley and the right-hand end of Quadrangle Support and sent his men forward at 9.00am.

In the German held trench Lieutenant Köstlin was waiting:

'During the morning', recorded Lieutenant Köstlin, *'The British made further effort to reach our trench by the sap (Quadrangle Alley) that came within 20 yards of our own left. My sentries, however, noticed steel helmets moving about above ground level at the sap head (trench block) and kept it under careful watch. Each time the men began to climb up out of the sap head and run forward at us with bombs, the sentries gave the alarm and we were able to greet them with heavy fire at point blank range. Then the others crowded at the sap head and repeated the effort, but with equal failure and by midday a heap of British dead and wounded lay about the sap head. Each time they had been checked, one of my men in particular ran forward across the open and threw bombs into the sap head and returned unhurt. The last time however, about midday he was shot before*

103

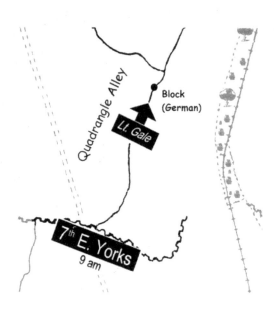

Map 17. Lieutenant Gales' attack on the German 'block' 10 July.

The position as described by Lieutenant Köstlin in Quadrangle Support Trench. Note how the trench lay conveniently behind the crest of a ridge. On the Left just forward of the bushes in the rough ground was the infamous 'block'. Further to the left and beyond is Quadrangle Wood. In this small area many brave British attackers perished. See Map 17

German belt buckle found in 1990 on the site of the battle. *Gott Mit Uns* (God with us).

he could get back.'

The attack by C company of the 7th East Yorks on the trench 'block' and junction was led by Lieutenant Gale, who reported every time an attempt was made to swarm across the 'block' the men were easily shot down. Major King seeing no progress by the 38th Division in the wood decided to suspend operations temporarily and await events from that direction.

Back with the 38th Division

Soon after 9.00am reports had come in that the Germans were reinforcing the northern end of the wood from the German main position in front of Bazentin Wood. A bombardment was organised to attempt to prevent this from continuing but being limited to only fifteen minutes was ineffective. At 10.30am Brigadier-General Marden put Lieutenant-Colonel Hayes in command of all troops of 114 Brigade on the right hand side of the wood with orders to push ahead to the second objective.

Because of overcrowding in the wood the 15th and 16th Royal Welsh Fusiliers were withdrawn. Also withdrawn from the wood was the remnants of the 14th Royal Welsh Fusiliers who were told to return to the railway cutting. They spent the time assisting the many wounded by giving water and first aid as best they could with many calling for help. Captain Glynn Jones recalled his sorrow and that "the circumstances were too tragic for description to one who had a share in the enlistment of and training of these men and who, in many cases, knew their people at home."

At 2.00pm an advance was made by 114 Brigade and the diary of the 10th Welsh records:

'At 2.00pm, the 10th had orders to advance to the 2nd objective which was done in 2 files of 2 companies each.

One file was strongly opposed by machine gun fire and sniping and returned to the trench to reorganise. This file again advanced after about 20 minutes and went through to the second objective.'

On the left, intense fire from Wood Support had still prevented any progress of the 113th Brigade now commanded by Brigadier-General Price-Davies and orders were sent from Major-General Watts at 38th

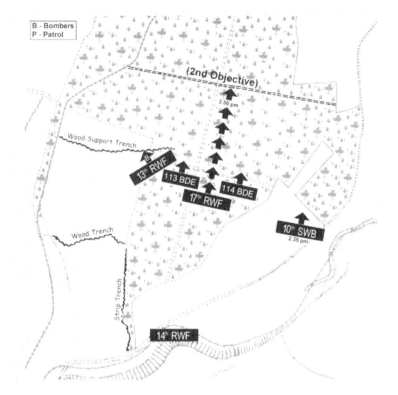

Map 18. The afternoon attack on the second objective 10 July.

Division Headquarters to try and work round to the trench and move forward without its capture. Price-Davies actually had a telephone that worked but could not make himself heard above the noise of battle.

Major-General Watts then decided to commit the 115th Brigade to the attack and two companies of the 10th South Wales Borderers and the 17th Royal Welsh Fusiliers moved forward to reinforce the 114th and the 113th Brigades respectively. The orders of the 10th South Wales Borderers given to them by Brigadier-General Marden at Brigade Headquarters were to go straight in and 'sweep through the wood' attacking the southern edge of the Hammerhead and clear it to the northern edge. A preliminary bombardment for half an hour was launched at 2.00pm and the attack got under way at 2.35pm. After only ten minutes though Colonel Hayes saw the officer commanding the 10th South Wales Borderers, Lieutenant-Colonel Harvey and told him to halt the attack and that a resumption would be made at 4.00pm.

The 17th Royal Welsh Fusiliers, the commanding officer Lieutenant-Colonel J A Ballard already a casualty, likewise, on the left at the lifting of the barrage attacked at approximately 2.30pm and fought their way forward with magnificent spirit as far as the second

Private H T Jenkins, 17 th Royal Welsh Fusiliers killed in action 11 July 1916. A bullet passed through his New Testament. His remains were lost and he is commerated on the Thiepval Memorial to the Missing of the Somme.

objective where they arrived at 3.50pm. Meanwhile Brigadier-General Marden went over to the wood from Brigade Headquarters and found that Brigadier-General Price-Davies and Lieutenant-Colonel H E ap Rhys-Price who had come from 38th Division Headquarters were arranging another assault at 4.30pm and to this he gave his support. Prior to this advance Price-Davies also made arrangements for the capture of Wood Support Trench bombers of the 13th Royal Welsh Fusiliers were to make the initial advance.

With the 17th Division

Back on the western side of the wood Lieutenant Köstlin was still established in Quadrangle Support Trench. He was no longer bothered by the British machine gun of the 8th South Staffs to his rear in Acid Drop Copse. That had been taken care of by a British shell which had landed directly on it killing all of the crew outright. He was able to concentrate on events in Mametz Wood and was surprised to see men of his regiment retiring from Wood Support Trench.

'I looked through my glasses. I looked again, it was incredible. But there he was, an Englishman in khaki and steel

Private Sam Robinson, 17th Battalion RWF killed at Mametz Wood 10 July.

Dear Mrs Robinson,

I hope you will forgive me for being so long in writing to you to offer my sincere sympathy. As you know Sam and I were deeply attached to each other and your loss is also my loss for I have lost a brave and good hearted chum. I do not know what to say to you as it all seems so strange. We were together just before we started on the charge but we soon got separated owing to the dense brushwood and broken branches. I thought no more, for it was every man for himself and then I saw J Roberts, the dark man who was with us. I said 'Hello Jack, hot isn't it'. He replied, 'Yes Sam has been killed'. I did not know what to think for it never entered my head that either of us would go under but we had no time to talk as the Germans were playing hell. So on we went and I paid them in full for I threw some bombs amongst them and then I got knocked out myself. I have been very lucky indeed and I only wish that Sam could have come through alright. He was a brave chap and one of the best and I shall always remember him. I must now close asking you to be brave and true and although you are denied the meeting on this earth yet remember that God ordained that all people shall meet in the Great Unknown. I am writing to some of the lads to know where he was buried and I will let you know.

helmet, standing bolt upright, regardless of cover as usual, near a long bare tree trunk. Looking more carefully, I saw others among the trees nearby. They must have broken through and come past our left flank under cover of the trees in the bed of the valley, and that explained the sudden withdrawal of the 5th and 9th Coys. I ordered fire to be opened on the patrol at the wood edge, and the men moved away into the cover. It did not alter the fact however, that Mametz Wood was now probably in British possession, threatening our line of retreat to Bazentin.'

Lieutenant Köstlin had fired on a forward patrol of the 6th Dorsets led by Lieutenant Clarke moving up the strip of woodland in the valley towards Wood Support Trench. After this action Lieutenant Clarke was listed as wounded and missing. Also watching these developments was Major King of the 7th East Yorks. He too saw German troops retreating from the western fringe of the wood and also British troops behind Wood Support Trench on the edge of the wood. He immediately fired

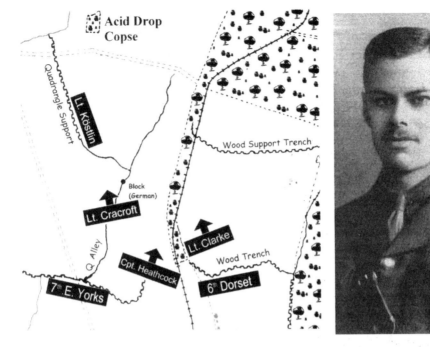

Map 19. Attempts by 17th Division to reach the south-west corner of Mametz Wood 10 July. Above: Lieutenant R B Cracroft

on the fleeing Germans and convinced the enemy was in retreat launched his second attack of the day, having received information that a bombing attack was to be made on the eastern end of Wood Support by the 38th Division. He had organised two platoons to be led by Lieutenant Cracroft to assault the junction by leaving Quadrangle Alley before the 'block' and rushing the trench over the open. Meanwhile Captain Heathcock would lead his men up the valley and to the western end of Wood Support with the south-west corner of Mametz Wood as the final objective.

The Germans had re-occupied Acid Drop Copse by now and as Lieutenant Cracroft charged the trench with his men he was met not only with fire from Lieutenant Köstlin's defenders but machine gun fire from the copse. Captain Heathcock advancing in extended order of two lines, came under machine gun fire from the western end of Wood Support and another at the south-west corner of Mametz Wood. Both attacks failed and both officers were killed, Captain Heathcock just as he reached the line of trees in the valley.

Lieutenant Köstlin recorded the attack led by Lieutenant Cracroft:

'Our ammunition was getting short, and we scraped together all we could find in the trench and the dug outs from the dead and wounded. Shortly afterwards a line of skirmishers suddenly

The view today from the position of Quadrangle Support Trench, Lieutenant Köstlin would have had of the line of trees, the clearing and Mametz Wood beyond.

appeared from a fold in the ground near the line of tall trees in the valley and advanced against the left of our trench. We were only just in time to stop them, the first extended line being shot down within a few yards of us. Already the second line was moving forward, and this was dealt with in the same way.

Fortunately, our old enemy in the sap had remained quiet after the lesson we had given him in the morning. an attack from there at this moment might well have been fatal for us.'

Lieutenant Köstlin did not realise that this attack was indeed made by his 'old enemy' the 7th East Yorks.

Major King seeing that there was no co-operation on his right called off his attack not feeling justified in sending in any more men. In his report he was clearly disappointed although he could not have been aware of the situation in the wood and the crisis caused by the loss of so many officers, he reported:

'Although all those British troops were in rear and right flank of the position and the enemy were clearly retiring, no attempt was made by them to co-operate with us, and I must state that I am convinced Wood Support could easily have been taken by them at that time while we were occupying the whole attention of the enemy by our attack.'

Lieutenant-Colonel Oswald S Flower, killed at Mametz Wood.

110

PART 2
The 38th Division Attacks Again

At 4.00pm the troops of the 38th Division had been reorganised and the advance through the wood was ready to commence.

The battalions leading the attack were as follows:

On the right the 10th South Wales Borderers were to attack the eastern portion of the wood and clear that portion of the Hammerhead not already in their possession. On their left was the 15th Welsh and continuing on their left was the 17th Royal Welsh Fusiliers. While on the extreme left were the 13th Royal Welsh Fusiliers whose bombers had been busy attacking the eastern end of Wood Support Trench. About fifty prisoners were taken and it was thought that the trench had been captured. However, this was not the case and considerable resistance was encountered at the western end before it finally fell to the attack of the 6th Dorsets much later in the evening. In close support behind these battalions were the 13th and 14th Welsh who were to advance up the central ride. All other battalions were held in reserve.

At 4.30pm the advance commenced from the second crossride; there was little opposition and progress was made by all battalions. On the right the 10 South Wales Borderers attacked the Hammerhead. In the centre the 15th Welsh and the 17th Royal Welsh Fusiliers also made an advance. On the left the 13th Royal Welsh Fusiliers still engaged at Wood Support Trench were left behind. The battalion had earlier lost its commanding officer and adjutant, both wounded by a British shell, and was now under the command of Captain Hardwick but shortly after 5.30pm made contact with the other attacking battalions. At about that time the commanding officer of the 13th Royal Welsh Fusiliers Lieutenant-Colonel Flower was severely wounded. He had worked tirelessly throughout to the point of exhaustion, even falling down and getting up again, determined to continue and refusing to retire. The damage was done by a British shell in a flat trajectory that hit the top

The valley along which Captain Heathcock attacked. He was killed just in front of the large clump of trees on the left. Mametz Wood on the right was protected by Wood trench and Wood Support Trench.

Private H E Evans, 10th South Wales Borderers was wounded in Mametz Wood and evacuated to England. While in hospital he was presented with the Military Medal for actions on 29 April 1916. He was killed in Salonika in 1918.

of the trees under which he was resting with his men just north of the intersection of the second crossride with the main ride.

The advance to the Northern perimeter of the wood continued; at about 6.30pm it reached within about forty yards of that objective when the attacking battalions came under heavy rifle and machine gun fire from Middle Alley a trench leading from the northern edge of the wood. During the confusion during which men retired under the fire Lewis gun crews of 113 Brigade Machine Gun Corps which had accompanied the attacking battalions were also caught up in the scramble. Second-Lieutenant Cullen though remained at his post with his gun and was cut off for some time. Before he could get back he was shot by his colleagues who advancing again mistook him in his isolated position for the enemy. In the advance, efforts to counter attack Middle Alley by the 14th Welsh and the 17th Royal Welsh Fusiliers were held up by thick undergrowth and they failed to get through in sufficient numbers although a bombing party led by Lieutenant Strange and Lieutenant Yorke made a determined effort to drive the Germans back down the trench and Lieutenant Rosser jumped out of the trench to try and throw bombs more effectively but was shot down. The troops were then all withdrawn to a line that varied in distance between 200 and 300 yards from the northern edge where digging in commenced.

In the rear the 13th Welsh sent forward their officers and a hundred men to assist with the consolidation. One of the officers was Second-Lieutenant Crossman who had earlier gone out on a patrol with Second-Lieutenant Purdie. Only when they arrived at the entrenching position was it realised that Second-Lieutenant Crossman was missing and a search failed to locate him.

A further attack was proposed at 8.00pm but by then the troops were exhausted and short of water and

Second Lieutenant G D M Crossman

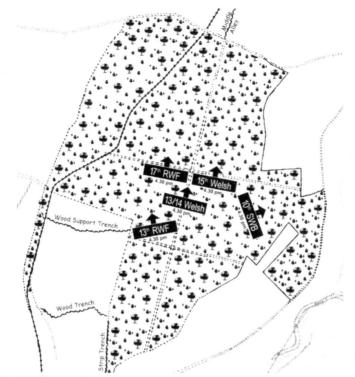

Map 20. The attack from the second cross ride 4.30pm 10 July.

this was abandoned. The men were very nervy and the slightest noise or disturbance brought a response of wild firing well into the early hours of 11 July. If the troops of the 38th Division were exhausted and short of water, unknown to them at that time the Germans too were in a sorry plight. Communication had been badly disrupted and no clear picture of the situation was available to any of the German commanders. In addition to taking heavy casualties over four hundred men had been captured and the only defenders left were one hundred and forty men .

That evening, having visited Lieutenant-General Horne at Heilly, Sir Douglas Haig was pleased with the news of the days events in Mametz Wood and no doubt, felt justified in his choice of Major-General Watts to command the 38th Division.

PART 3
A Last Effort by the 17th Division

Major King was still in Quadrangle Alley with the 7th East Yorks and at 6.45pm again seeing British troops at the back of Wood Support Trench ordered one more attack in an attempt to reach his objective at the south-west corner of Mametz Wood. Another assault was to be made on the western end of Wood Support and in addition half of B Company was sent forward up the valley towards the south-western corner of the wood. This was led by Lieutenant Goodwin who came under fire from two machine guns in Acid Drop Copse and another at the end of Wood Support Trench which his attacking colleagues could not dislodge.

Unknown to Major King ten minutes before he attacked a message had been received at 17th Division Headquarters that the Germans had been seen withdrawing from Quadrangle Support Trench. Some Germans were, indeed, withdrawing, but had left the strong points and machine gun positions manned.

Lieutenant Köstlin remained in Quadrangle Support Trench in spite of the flight of some of the German troops and easily repelled the attack led by Lieutenant Goodwin.

His report goes on:

'But the surprises of the day were not at an end. Whilst searching with my glasses, there suddenly appeared in the big open clearing in Mam. Wood - across which was Wood Support Trench, lines of skirmishers who advanced across the open directly against Wood Support. From that trench came no sound, it seemed that both the 5th and 9th Coys had vanished into space. Nevertheless from our trench the advancing lines offered an excellent target, as we were in a position to enfilade them at a range of 600 yards. I scarcely needed to give the order. My men had already seen the target, and a rapid fire opened almost at once. Every rifle was at work, the officers picking up rifles and joining in, until soon all the rifle barrels were red hot. Not a single Englishman seemed to reach Wood Support Trench, and a large no. lay dead and wounded about the open clearing .....
From the firing in the wood it was evident that we had only held up the left flank guard of the main force advancing through the wood itself.'

Lieutenant Köstlin had witnessed an attack on Wood Support Trench by the 6th Dorsets. It will be recalled that under the command of Major Hughes-Onslow the Dorsets had occupied Wood Trench and had held it since the evening of 8 July. At 11.00am on 10 July they had lost their acting commanding officer when he was killed by a stray bullet. Captain O'Hanlon took over and later that evening made one more assault on the strongly defended western end of the trench.

The German officer was mistaken in thinking that none of the 6th Dorsets reached their objective. The assault was led by Lieutenant

Davidson who took the same route as the patrol fired on earlier by Lieutenant Köstlin, along the valley and up to the western edge of Wood Support Trench. While many men fell in front of Wood Support Lieutenant Davidson and some men entered the trench and captured the strongly fortified 'block' and then fought down the trench towards the wood. Lieutenant Davidson was twice wounded but was eventually evacuated. A report was received at 10.55pm at 17th Division Headquarters that Wood Support Trench had been finally occupied.

News had also been received of the capture of Contalmaison by the 23rd Division and orders were issued for the 10th Sherwood Foresters who had relieved the 8th South Staffordshires in Quadrangle Trench to attack Quadrangle Support Trench, together with the 7th Lincolns supported by the 8th South Staffordshires. Lieutenant-Colonel Bunbury commanding the Sherwood Foresters after consulting the 7th Lincolns ordered the attack to commence at 9.45pm. After a bombardment the battle patrols and Lewis gun crews advanced and attacked under a heavy enemy counter barrage. The trench was occupied. On the right the 7th Green Howards relieving the exhausted 7th East Yorks later pushed patrols up Quadrangle Alley to the 'block' and the junction of Quadrangle Support. The only occupants of the trench were two wounded Northumberland Fusiliers in the company of some wounded Germans in a deep dugout. Lieutenant Köstlin and the remnants of his defending companies had slipped away under cover of their machine guns once they realised that the 38th Division were making progress on their left and Contalmaison had fallen on the right.

Major D Hughes-Onslow

Lieutenant G C Davidson

'The ground behind our trench was being continually shelled but about midnight the fire ceased and we decided to rush for it. The plan worked successfully and although a number of men were wounded by shells and stray bullets we succeeded, a total of five officers and 120 men, in reaching the barbed wire

*entanglements in front of the second line position at 1.30am.
Here we were greeted by a machine gun which suddenly opened
from the trench, but throwing ourselves on the ground and
shouting we soon convinced the gunner of his error and luckily
with no cost to ourselves.'*

The last recorded casualty of the 17th Division was Lieutenant Kimber of the 7th Lincolns who together with Lieutenant Barrett, it will be recalled, successfully led the first battle patrols of their battalion into Fricourt village on the 2 July. Lieutenant Kimber was killed by shellfire when the 6th Lincolns advanced. His colleague, Lieutenant Barrett had been wounded on the 3 July in the attack on Railway Alley and died the following day. The 17th Division had been due to be relieved by the 21st Division on the night of the 10/11 July and this duly took place.

Major-General Pilcher at least had the satisfaction of seeing his men in occupation of Quadrangle Support Trench, even if it was at such a cost. In the period from 1 July to 11 July the Division lost 197 officers and 4,574 other ranks (91 officers and 1,634 other ranks killed or missing). Only part of 50 Brigade had attacked on the 1 July and although the 10th West Yorks suffered the highest number of casualties by any battalion on that day with (710 of which 396 were killed) the great majority of the Division's casualties were, therefore, incurred in the push towards Quadrangle Support Trench between 2 - 10 July.

A message was sent at 7.45am on the 11 July from XV Corps Headquarters to 17th Division Headquarters requesting Major-General Pilcher to go to Heilly to see Lieutenant-General Horne as soon as he had finished handing over to the 21st Division. Later that day Pilcher's military career was effectively over when he was relieved of his command.

On 13 July a special order was issued to the 17th Division which stated:

*'On giving up command of the 17th Division Major-General
T D Pilcher wishes to thank all ranks for the invariable support
they have given him and for the magnificent work which they
have always done.*

*He wishes the Division every good fortune and hopes it will
add laurels to the fame it has already gained.'*

It was rather a sad end for a soldier who had a long and creditable career in the service of his country

Chapter Seven

THE FINAL HOURS
10/11 July

Late into the evening of the 10 July the 10th South Wales Borderers had continued their efforts to secure the Hammerhead. All but the northern part had been captured and scouts sent out reported that a trench ran along the eastern edge with machine gun posts at its most northerly point. Four attempts were made to capture the position. Firstly by bombing up the trench where the assaulting bombers were driven back. A second attempt was made in waves formation through the wood but they too suffered heavily. Two more bombing attacks from different positions were also repulsed before darkness fell and the troops dug in for the night near the second crossride. In the dark a patrol was sent out into the open east of the wood and located another trench that ran from Flat Iron Copse into the Hammerhead just where the machine guns were situated. A strong picquet was put over the trench to cut off the Germans in the wood and at dawn Lieutenant-Colonel Harvey gave orders for a simultaneous attack on both flanks. By 5.30am the attack had succeeded and the Hammerhead was in the possession of the Welsh. Twenty four prisoners were taken and several field guns had been captured.

At 5.00am on 11 July Brigadier-General Evans, who had instigated the curtailment of the disastrous attack on the Hammerhead on 7 July arrived in the wood to take over command. He brought with him the remainder of 115 Brigade.

After the relief Evans reorganised the battalions. Along the railway line on the left were the 16th Royal Welsh Fusiliers and continuing along the railway on the right the 16th Welsh. In the centre were the 17th Royal Welsh Fusiliers and on their right the 11th South Wales Borderers. Finally as we have seen on the extreme right in the Hammerhead were the 10th South Wales Borderers.

Evans thought the wood to had been captured and was not expecting to have to make another attack. He immediately set out reconnoitring the wood with the assistance of Brigadier-General Marden from whom he was taking over command. Also accompanying him was Lieutenant-Colonel J R Gaussen commanding the 11th South Wales Borderers and a party of bayonet men. Gaussen recalled later that they lost their way and blundered on to the northern edge of the wood but were not fired on. A little later they were talking in whispers when the British artillery

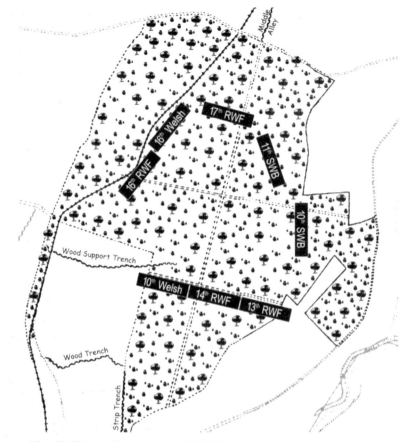

Map 21. The position morning of 11 July.

opened up on the northern part of the wood. A shrapnel shell burst overhead and killed eight out of the eleven bayonet men and wounded Major Veal who was Brigade-Major of 115 Brigade in the leg.

Evans who had been wounded in the arm sent for Captain Griffith who after giving assistance to Evans on 7 July had been made acting Staff-Captain to 115 Brigade as the original officer had become a casualty. Captain Griffith's journey through the wood was a memorable one and is vividly recorded in his book *Up to Mametz.*

'Men of my battalion were lying dead on the ground in great profusion... There were more corpses than men but there were worse sights than corpses. Limbs and mutilated trunks, here and there a detached head forming splashes of red against the green leaves... Blue sky above a band of green trees and a ploughed graveyard in which living men moved in and out of sight: three men digging a trench thigh deep in the red soil, digging their own graves, as it chanced, for a bursting shell turned their

118

A Brigadier General consults with other officers in Mametz Wood.

shelter into a tomb.'

Captain Griffith was to take over the duties of Brigade-Major. He arrived and was greeted by the signals officer Lieutenant Taylor. Brigadier-General Evans continued his reconnaissance and strengthened and consolidated the front line. He reported to Major-General Watts at 9.10am explaining that the whole position was still somewhat unstable. Watt's reply received at 11.40am by Evans was uncompromising. He was told to make an attack. Watts told him that the Germans had no strong force and that a determined attack with only a few men should clear the wood that day.

At about the same time a staff officer arrived and gave orders to make an attack on the north and west edges of the wood. When the

Sergeant J Richards, 15th Battalion Welsh Regiment, was wounded in Mametz Wood. While doing some wiring in the wood his right hand was around a tree and a sniper put five bullets into it. It was subsequently amputated, and a hook replaced the hand. On leaving the army he worked in the mines where an accident caused his hook to seriously injure his leg, which then had to be amputated at Cardiff Hospital. The ward where he recovered was, coincidently, the Mametz Memorial Ward.

staff officer had finished Evans told him he was in no position to make an attack and he did not intend to do so until in his judgement it was appropriate. In that event he was going to make a surprise attack with the bayonet and he did not require an artillery bombardment to announce to the Germans that the attack was imminent.

Messages were being sent by runners and Evans also asked the staff officer on his return to tell 38th Divisional Headquarters that he did not want a barrage prior to the attack which he fixed for 3.00pm. This information must have got through to Divisional Headquarters as the diary records that at '12.50pm orders were issued by the G.O.C. 115 Brigade for an attack at 3.00pm'. Thereafter things did not go according to plan for Evans.

Prior to the attack all units sent out patrols to locate the German position. The western side of the wood was reported clear but the Germans had re-occupied the northern edge and set up several machine gun positions. At 2.45pm just fifteen minutes before the attack a massive British artillery barrage opened up on the northern edge of the wood. Many shells fell short and the awaiting troops took many casualties. Evans immediately postponed the attack and ordered it to proceed only on the cessation of the bombardment. With all telephone communication still lost it was impossible to stop the barrage except by runners. Evans was dismayed and ordered Griffith to send a message. Three runners set off by different routes to try and get to Queen's Nullah. The Germans responded with their own counter-barrage and the wood was a storm of shells. Over half an hour later this had still not relented and Lieutenant Taylor despatched a further three runners. At 3.30pm the British barrage lifted.

Some of the battalions were badly shaken the 16th Welsh in particular, reported many casualties and the advance was disrupted, especially on the left.The Adjutant, Captain Harris, was carried back, dying, by Doctor Pettigrew so that he should not be lost, to whom he gave his wedding ring to pass on in turn to Major Angus who was to return it to his wife whom he had married the previous October.

The 16th Royal Welsh Fusiliers pushed out patrols at the cessation of the barrage but the major part of the battalion held the line and did not advance until 6.00pm. Likewise on their right the 16th Welsh made no significant advance because of the weakness in numbers of the 17th Royal Welsh Fusiliers on their right who had attempted to get forward in the face of heavy machine gun fire on the right. The 11th South Wales Borderers also moved forward but found the going through the undergrowth and damaged trees desperately hard. Only two companies made the advance another two being left in the Hammerhead.

Captain L A P Harris knew he was dying and sent his wedding ring back to his wife, Mary, who remarried within six months.

A British patrol sets off into the tangled undergrowth.

Lieutenant-Colonel Gaussen commanding the 11th South Wales Borderers acting on his own initiative amalgamated detachments of the 10th South Wales Borderers to reinforce his own battalion. Reporting later, he realised the commanding officer of that battalion had become a casualty and also that Brigadier-General Evans, short of staff officers, had sustained a further wound this time to the head and was weakened through loss of blood. A Company of the 11th South Wales Borderers fought its way forward through the machine gun fire and in hand to hand combat and eventually reached the north eastern corner of the wood. B Company made slower progress but later arrived at the northern edge of the wood on the left of A Company and consolidated to within about seventy five yards of Middle Alley which was still occupied by Germans. It was through this trench that the Germans had been able to reinforce the wood overnight and during the morning of the 11 July with a thousand men.

Meanwhile on the extreme left the 10th Welsh who were in support at the first objective were quickly brought forward and advanced at 4.00pm ahead of the 16th Royal Welsh Fusiliers and the 16th Welsh who were still dug in. At 6.00pm these two battalions also moved forward. At precisely the same time the Germans unleashed a barrage of 5.9 howitzer shells on the attacking battalions.

The 10th Welsh, however, progressed to within forty yards of the

The Hardwidge brothers. Tom, the eldest, was hit by a sniper's bullet and when Henry went to his assistance he was also hit whilst giving his brother a drink of water. They died in each others arms and are buried together in Flat Iron Copse Cemetery.

western edge of the wood. They were joined by the 16th Royal Welsh Fusiliers and elements of the 15th Welsh also in support who found the ground ahead of them abandoned by the Germans. One platoon of the 16th Royal Welsh Fusiliers was then able to penetrate into the north western portion of the wood. Additional machine guns had been brought in by Captain Job leading 115 Brigade Machine Gun Company. During the advance Captain Job assisted by Second-Lieutenant Southon captured some German troops during which action one of the prisoners was shot by Captain Job before the situation was under control.

German *flammenwerfer* in action.

In the centre the 16th Welsh were also able to advance with remnants of the 17th Royal Welsh Fusiliers but could not get to the northern edge of the wood owing to a *flammenwerfer* attack and they consolidated about sixty yards inside the perimeter where they attempted to hold on. This left the 11th South Wales Borderers who, it will be remembered, had successfully captured the north western part of the wood open to attack on their left flank. No reinforcements were forthcoming and there was no alternative but to withdraw and Lieutenant-Colonel Gaussen reluctantly retired with his exhausted men under the heavy bombardment which caused more casualties than had been suffered in hand to hand fighting during the advance.

PART 2

At 12.00 midday the 14th Royal Welsh Fusiliers had been ordered back into the wood to the first objective where they waited until 4.00pm when further orders came to move forward to support the 11th South Wales Borderers. With only Captain Glynn Jones and Sergeant Thompson leading them, they soon got lost and were eventually fired on from the left. Glynn Jones decided to dig in and later some men of the 13th Royal Welsh Fusiliers arrived led by Captain Hardwick. Also additional units of the 14th Royal Welsh Fusiliers arrived under Captain Wheldon. The only contact made with the 11th South Wales Borderers was on the right when some of their men were seen retiring but from whom they were unable to get any information. The position they held, according to the battalion diary, was fifty yards from the edge of the wood, but exactly which edge of the wood is not stated and their exact position not known. At 10.00pm Captain Glynn Jones reported to Brigadier-General Evans and was ordered to retire to the position of the first objective where they remained until midnight when the battalion was relieved.

Meanwhile the 16th Welsh and the 17th Royal Welsh Fusiliers in the centre could not hold on and at 9.20pm they fell back to their original position.

At 10.50pm the troops on the left in the north western portion of the wood were subjected to heavy artillery and trench mortar fire. The men were compelled to fall back to the line of the railway from which they had attacked at 3.30pm. Thereby all troops had retired to the positions from which they had attacked. Among the casualties was Captain Job killed by a shell by the railway line at the south western corner of the wood. In one final gesture of defiance at 11.20pm the Germans opened fire with rifles and machine guns on the Welshmen, probably in an attempt to locate their positions. There was no response from the exhausted troops and the Germans contented themselves with shelling the wood throughout the night.

Earlier that day the 21st Division had been ordered to take over. It was not possible, however, to make the relief during the daylight although Lewis gun crews of the 12th Northumberland Fusiliers set out from Meaulte as early as midday and later that afternoon entered Mametz Wood by the central ride. The officer and sergeant in charge halted the men on the ride and went forward themselves to locate 115 Brigade. Among the men was Corporal Fellows of C Company in charge of two Lewis guns. While waiting he and Private Templeton decided to go and look for some souvenirs, for which there was a lucrative trade behind the lines, especially such items as German watches and Iron Crosses and other medals.

While they were away four shells fell in the vicinity of the waiting troops and they hurriedly returned to find over half the complement of fifty men dead or wounded. They sent a wounded man back for stretcher bearers and picking up two Lewis guns went forward to find the officer and sergeant. They stumbled over the numerous dead in the wood and seeing no-one arrived at the northern perimeter of the wood about fifty yards to the left of the central ride. Calling out they moved to the right and eventually found three men of the 10th South Wales Borderers in a shell hole with a Lewis gun in the north-east part of the wood. The 10th South Wales Borderers had already retired but left the gun to cover and wait for relief. Two of the Welshmen left taking their gun with them but the third was wounded and dying. He was duly buried by the two Northumberland Fusiliers in the shell hole in which he had been lying who were surprised to find that the South Wales Borderer was in fact a Scotsman. At dusk the Germans shelled the front of the wood and the two men moved to a shell hole about thirty yards in front of the wood. As daylight approached sounds of digging came from the wood behind them as their colleagues arrived. They could not move back, however, as the Germans had two snipers in Bazentin Wood in front of them pinning them down.

The relief by the 21st Division took most of the night of the 11/12 July. One of the last battalions to move out was the 10th South Wales Borderers whose commanding officer Lieutenant-Colonel Harvey recorded his relief in the Hammerhead by the 7th Green Howards at 7.00am.

As darkness fell Lieutenant Taylor the signals officer had sought the whereabouts of Captain Griffith.

'I want to have a word with you' he said drawing me away
'I've got bad news for you ...'
'Whats happened to my young brother ... is he hit?'
'You know the last message you sent to try to stop the barrage ...well he was one of the runners that took it. He hasn't come back ... He got the message through all right and on the way back through the barrage he was hit. His mate was wounded by the shell that killed your brother... he told another runner to tell us'
'My God, ... he's lying out there now Taylor!'
'No old man ... He's gone'
'Yes ... Yes he's gone'
'I'm sorry ...I had to send him you know'
'Yes of course ...you had to. I can't leave this place ... I suppose there's no doubt about him being killed?'
'None... he's out of it now.'
So I had sent him to his death bearing a message from my own hand in an endeavour to save other mens' brothers. Night came I could not sleep. At two in the morning we set out to join the battalion and as the dawn was breaking over Bazentin I turned towards the green shape of Mametz Wood and shuddered in a farewell to one, to many. I had not even buried him nor was his grave ever found.'

As we know Private David Jones too survived the battle to tell of his experiences but not before he had been wounded.

Unable to walk he had dragged himself back through the wood holding on at all costs, as all soldiers were very strictly commanded, to his rifle.

'It's difficult with the weight of the rifle. Leave it – under the oak. Leave it for a salvage-bloke. Slung so, it swings its full weight. With you going blindly on all paws, it slews its whole length, to hang at your bowed neck like the mariner's white oblation. You drag past the four bright stones at the turn of Wood Support. It is not to be broken on the brown stone under the gracious tree. It is not to be hidden under your failing body. Slung so, it troubles your painful crawling like a fugitive's irons. At the gate of the wood you try a last adjustment but slung so, it's an impediment, it's of detriment to your hopes, you had best be rid of it – the sagging webbing and all and what's left of your two fifty – but it were wise to hold on to your mask. You're clumsy in your feebleness, you implicate your tin-hat rim with the slack sling of it. Let it lie for the dews to rust it, or ought you to decently cover the working parts. Its dark barrel, where you leave it under the oak, reflects the solemn star that rises urgently from Cliff Trench. It's a beautiful doll for us it's the Last Reputable Arm. But leave it – under the oak. Leave it for a Cook's tourist to the Devastated Areas and crawl as far as you can and wait for the bearers.'

The total number of casualties sustained by the 38th Welsh Division were:

	Officers	Other Ranks
Killed	46	556
Missing	6	579
Wounded	138	2668
	190	3803

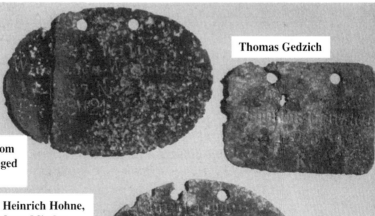

German identity tags found near Mametz Wood.

Thomas Gedzich

Willi Diel, from Wiesbaden aged nineteen

Heinrich Hohne, from Minden aged twenty-two

Chapter Eight

AFTER THE BATTLE

The units of the 21st Division which relieved the 38th Welsh Division in the wood were the 12th and 13th Northumberland Fusiliers, the 1st Lincolnshire Regiment and the 10th Green Howards. These battalions comprised the strength of 62 Brigade. They set out at 7.15pm to reach the wood and the two battalions of the Northumberland Fusiliers were deployed in the front line. On the left, the western side of the central ride were the 13th Northumberland Fusiliers while in the centre and towards the eastern side were the 12th Northumberland Fusiliers. The Germans continued to shell the wood throughout the relief and the 1st Lincolns in support reached the wood at 3.00am, entering the wood through Strip Trench which was difficult to negotiate because of the large number of German dead. Two companies deployed into Wood Trench with two further companies dug in the central part of the wood.

Meanwhile the two battalions of the Northumberland Fusiliers immediately began digging in and also pushed out patrols to establish the enemy's position and strength. The 13th Northumberland Fusiliers pushed the remaining Germans back and out of the wood, and the front line was reformed on the western and north-western edge of the wood. Even less resistance was encountered by the 12th Northumberland Fusiliers who found only isolated groups of Germans who offered only half-hearted resistance. The front line was established thirty yards from the northern edge of the wood. Corporal Fellows and Private Templeton who had been pinned down all day in front of the wood were only able to rejoin their battalion at dusk on the 12 July when they got back the company commander exclaimed 'Where the hell have you come from?' Both had been reported as 'Missing in Action'. The 1st Lincolns and 10th Green Howards were not called forward to assist but a large shell landed directly in Wood Trench and wiped out a whole company of the 1st Lincolns.

At dawn on the morning of 13 July the Germans made a heavy counter attack on the positions held by 13th Northumberland Fusiliers. This was eventually driven off and twelve prisoners were taken. During the period that the Northumberland Fusiliers held the front of the wood between 11 and 17 July they suffered the following casualties. The 13th Northumberland Fusiliers 43 killed and 227 wounded. The 12th

Scene in Death Valley – troops shelter from exploding shells.

Northumberland Fusiliers were less effected having a total of eighty casualties of all ranks killed and wounded. The majority of these casualties were caused by shell fire. The way was now clear for the planned assault on the German second line between Bazentin-le-Petit Wood and Longueval and during the struggle ahead the ground over which the 38th Division attacked, became known as Death Valley. It was one of the major supply routes to the front line and as such attracted considerable attention from the German artillery.

Soon after the capture of the wood Lieutenant-Colonel R W Castle of 79 Brigade Royal Field Artillery was ordered to take his brigade into Death Valley. He reconnoitred the battery positions and went into Mametz Wood where he found trenches full of dead Germans. Passing through the wood into the valley he found men of the 38th Division lying thickly on the ground outside the wood, not yet buried. There was heavy shelling and he got to the place where he was supposed to put his guns and found it one mass of bursting shells. He could see nothing but smoke and dust. Realising that it was useless to attempt to put the guns in the valley he selected a quieter place south of Mametz Wood instead; much to the relief of his battery commanders.

Another officer who went into the wood after the battle was Lieutenant-Colonel M J F Fitzgerald of 95 Brigade Royal Field Artillery. On 15 July he was ordered to report on the number and kind of guns the Germans had left in the wood. He explored a deep German dugout with his orderly officer. They had no torch and to find the way they struck matches and lit paper. With revolvers in hand they crept along and hearing a noise found a wounded German who shrieked 'Kamerad' in terror, lying on a shelf with his leg badly smashed.

128

The same scene in the 1990s.

Neither officer could speak German but understood his fear to be caused because he had been told the British shot their prisoners. He had been without food and water for three days and though they had no water they gave him some biscuits and chocolate. Returning to the top of the dugout Lieutenant-Colonel Fitzgerald organised medical assistance.

The British artillery did manage to establish themselves both in Mametz Wood and in Death Valley and also in Caterpillar Valley. Lieutenant-Colonel Castle finally got his gun positions established and Lieutenant-Colonel Fitzgerald later recorded that Caterpillar Valley was a remarkable sight soon covered with 18 pounder and 4.5″ Howitzer batteries. Several lines of guns were separated by only 300 yards distance and an occasional premature detonation occurred causing casualties. On one occasion a howitzer shell detonated prematurely and killed the whole gun detachment while later in the same day another howitzer suffered a direct hit from a German shell also killing every man in its detachment.

Gun positions were also established forward of Mametz Wood. Some 4.5″ Howitzers and 18 pounder field batteries were positioned in a hollow near the north-west corner of Mametz Wood. Nearly all were put out of action by salvoes of 5.9″ Howitzer shells which burst with uncanny accuracy. The reason for this became apparent when Lieutenant-Colonel Fitzgerald was visiting 101 Brigade Headquarters and a German artillery officer was brought in. He had been hiding in the south-eastern corner of Bazentin Wood for three days after its capture on 14 July with a telephone and was able to organise fire on to the British positions by direct observation.

There were other less acceptable reasons for casualties. Lieutenant-Colonel Castle was ordered to carry out a relief in daylight. The German air reconnaissance was very active over the wood and the valley and they soon spotted this movement. Many of the men of both brigades were casualties from the resulting shell-fire.

Robert Graves also wrote of his experience in Mametz Wood in his autobiography *Goodbye to all That*. His battalion, 2nd Royal Welsh Fusiliers (23rd Division) was in reserve and bivouacking near the wood. On the night of 16 July he was cold and went into the wood looking for German greatcoats to use as blankets. He stayed as briefly as he was able in the circumstances among the dead and mutilated bodies of Welshmen and Germans, the smashed trees and broken branches. He wrote of the unforgettable sight of a 'South Wales Borderer and a German soldier of the Lehr Regiment who had bayoneted each other simultaneously.'

A few days later the 2nd Royal Welsh Fusiliers moved forward to the attack on the German second position. On 20 July they were in reserve to an attack by units of the 7th Division on High Wood. Waiting near the village cemetery in Bazentin-le-Petit shells were landing uncomfortably close by. It was decided to move back a further fifty yards to a relatively safer location. As he moved Graves was hit by a shell which burst just behind him. He was wounded in his upper left thigh but was more seriously a shard of metal had entered his back by the right shoulder and was protruding through his chest. He was taken back to Mametz Wood and into an old German dugout where he lay unconscious for over twenty four hours. Lieutenant-Colonel Crawshay his commanding officer was told that there was no hope for his survival and wrote a letter of condolence to his mother. On the 21 July when the dead were being removed Graves was found to be still breathing and was put on an ambulance to be taken to Heilly and to survive his wounds. The journey down Death Valley was extremely difficult and painful, the vehicle jolting him out of unconsciousness as it passed over shell holes every few yards.

There are many accounts and descriptions of the wood and the valley and most make mention of the general devastation and death that had prevailed the evidence of which was still very much apparent. This type of warfare was different and it was obvious to all that something particularly unusual and unpleasant had occurred there. Similar scenes would re-emerge in all of the dark woods of Picardy but the concentration of death and destruction in such a limited timescale would never be surpassed.

Yet another author, Gerald Brennan had a similar experience to Graves and wrote of the incredible sight of two soldiers still standing having fallen against a tree but locked together by their bayonets while all around them the shattered remains of the wood and the dead were lying just as they had fallen as if in 'an exhibit for a war museum.'

The following weeks extended into months and Death Valley was the constant scene of winding columns of guns, ammunition, supplies and troops. The guns of the British continued to launch barrage after barrage. The Germans responded and the ambulances continued to convey their burdens down the valley.

Private William Ballard, Welsh Regiment, died of wounds received at Mametz Wood. His parents came from England and his father worked all over the country on Brunel's tunnels, finally settling in Swansea. From a family of eight children, four brothers and the father joined the army. All except William returned. A sister still lives in Swansea and relatives from Pembroke still visit the grave in Flat Iron Copse Cemetery.

Following the relief of the 38th Division Major-General Watts returned to the 7th Division and Major-General Blackader finally took over the division which after a brief spell near the end of July in the front line at Serre, Redan Ridge and Beaumont-Hamel, moved away from the Somme and did not return to the battle. This has been used as a basis to imply that the division was in some kind of disgrace and there is some evidence of this.

One of the strongest critics initially was Brigadier-General Price-Davies who, it will be recalled witnessed the withdrawal in some panic of some men of the division when he went into the wood on the morning of 10 July. The congestion and confusion he encountered later must have added to this negative view of things. He felt that 'we should recognise and face our failure' but later relented and wrote what amounts to a retraction of his report.

'since then I have had the accounts of certain gallant actions performed by officers and other ranks and I feel that possibly I may not have given my Brigade full credit for what they did in Mametz Wood... Further, from rumours which reach me, I believe other troops operating in High Wood, Bois du Trones found it extremely difficult to organise an advance under such conditions. I realise it is now too late to add to any account which has been sent forward ...'

By 20 July though, the day he wrote these sentiments, it would indeed have been too late to effect much damage limitation.

Some days previously Second Lieutenant Siegfried Sassoon wrote of 'wild rumours' that reached the camp about the Welsh Division stampeding under machine gun fire. Perhaps Sassoon's choice of words betrays his belief in the veracity of such talk and he quickly dismisses the subject preferring to concentrate on his eagerly awaited outing to Amiens.

It was retirements as witnessed by Brigadier-General Price-Davies that similarly affected Captain Glynn Jones who recorded that he was staggered to find that when he arrived back at rear headquarters with his relatively small party of men, many others were already there, having 'found their way in the early stages'. Captain Glynn Jones goes on to state that the division did not please and that recommendations for awards were not considered in the same manner as those affecting very much simpler operations.

A further strong critic was to emerge some years later when responding to requests for information from the Official Historian in 1930 Major G P L Drake-Brockman wrote at length about both the 17th and the 38th Division. His main target was Major-General Phillips from whom, he alleged, all the problems of the division issued. Phillips, he claimed was 'ignorant lacked experience and failed to inspire confidence...' 'an influential political atmosphere permeated the whole division and was the cause of considerable friction.'

Drake-Brockman transferred from the 7th Division Headquarters to the staff of 38th Division on 8 July. As we know Major-General Phillips left the division in the early hours of 9 July, not a very long time for Drake-Brockman to establish a basis for his assertions which must therefore be largely based on hearsay. Not that that necessarily invalidates all he had to say, but further caution should be observed since some of Drake-Brockman's claims are factually inaccurate, for example when he states that the death of Lieutenant-Colonel Carden largely contributed to Phillip's dismissal. As we have seen Phillips had already left when Carden was killed on 10 July.

Drake-Brockman completes his deposition to the official historian by claiming that the 'stigma' of Mametz Wood stuck to the 38th Division for many months and that it was common talk in the B.E.F. that the division had 'bolted'. In looking further at Drake-Brockman's credibility it is difficult to imagine as a junior officer he could have been at the centre of, and had access to all the reports, comment and opinions, official or otherwise that he claims was so widespread. After all, the 38th Division were removed from the environs of the Somme soon after and communications then were not as we enjoy and take for granted today.

There remains, though, the core accusation that in panic some men left the immediate scene of battle in some disarray. That it occurred cannot be denied but before condemning any instances of this conduct it is important to try and somehow re-create the situation and understand the conditions in the wood as far as that is possible. It is interesting to look back a few day when a frustrated Brigadier-General Evans was prevented by XV Corps from assembling his troops in the concentration that he considered appropriate to capture the Hammerhead. He was ordered not to use any more battalions than

Wrecked German transport at the edge of Mametz Wood. TAYLOR LIBRARY

absolutely necessary and to avoid risk of casualties from shell-fire by dispersing supporting battalions. All this seems to have been forgotten when Major-General Watts planned the second assault on 10 July. Seven battalions were soon to be engaged in what is the smallest part of the wood and in all eleven battalions were employed in the operation. This might be described in today's terminology as 'overkill' and a glaring inconsistency in tactics and strategy.

Casualties among the officers was very heavy and there was a great shortage, very necessary for rallying, re-organising and steadying the men at a critical time. Many men were left leaderless, men whose first taste of action this was and in a situation that would have tested the most battle hardened troops. Enfiladed from both flanks, by machine gun fire from the Quadrangle and from Sabot and Flat Iron Copses as well as frontal fire the troops were also caught in two bombardments, the German and the British detonating in the tree tops. As the shells detonated they would send lethal sprays of shrapnel flying through the air and into the trees and undergrowth. We are told that the sound of this factor alone was enough to unnerve some of the troops. Then there would be the high explosive shells detonating with jagged shards of hot metal impacting with great velocity sending splinters of wood hurtling through the air. The trees themselves would be splintering and falling on top of the troops. Those shells that found their way through the foliage would land with an massive explosion throwing huge mounds of earth into the air and burying many men both dead and alive. The flammenwerfer was also used and parts of the wood would be scorched by fire. This then might be something like, just a snapshot of the whole picture in Mametz Wood and the probability of certain death for anyone unwise enough to stay around for too long waiting for someone to tell them what to do.

David Jones was able to say everything in just those few words

'... and but we avoid wisely there is but death.'

Of death there was plenty. Those who later passed could only conclude that here was incontrovertible evidence that anything but a retreat had taken place. Many years later a survivor of the battle described the men of the 38th Division as 'civilians in uniform.' Nevertheless, they were able, through the capture of Mametz Wood in three days of actual fighting, to set the standard for this type of combat that was never to be surpassed on the Somme Battlefields.

THE GENERALS

The attacks on the Quadrangle and Mametz Wood are unusual in as much as that they resulted in the two divisions concerned both having their commanders removed. The generals could not have been more different.

Major-General T D Pilcher was born in 1858 and was a soldier of distinction who was first commissioned in the Northumberland Fusiliers at the age of twenty one. He saw considerable service abroad in West Africa, South Africa and India. In South Africa he commanded the 3rd Corps M.I. for a period and at a time when things were not going well he obtained a much needed victory, which was not as significant as its subsequent popularity in the British press. Nevertheless Pilcher's name was familiar in many households. He was promoted Major-General in 1907 and later appointed an A.D.C. to King George V. He was given command of the 17th Division in January 1915 but, as with many others in his position, found mechanised warfare quite different to his previous experience. As we have seen he was prepared to question his orders and press his argument to the limit.

It is also possible that at the age of fifty eight he found the pressure in Divisional Headquarters too great. Writing after the war, Brigadier-General R J Collins, who was then attached to the 17th Division as a staff officer recorded that the average working day could be up to eighteen hours and implies that Pilcher's demise was as much the result of exhaustion as his unpopularity at XV Corps Headquarters.

Pilcher himself, writing after the war, admits he had no appetite, for some of the tasks he was ordered to perform and finding himself ordered to repeat a frontal attack in broad daylight immediately following the failure of a night time assault wrote:

'I protested... and begged to be allowed to confine my operations to a bombing attack, but the reply I received was a definite command to make a frontal attack. For several minutes I pondered and once again took up the telephone with the object of informing the corps that I must refuse to carry out that order, and begged to resign my command. Then I thought that the only consequence of such action would be that someone else would be put in my place and would probably carry out the operation in such a manner that far greater losses would be incurred than if I were to undertake it myself, and I issued orders in accordance with the instructions I had received, employing a minimum

number of men. If four times as many had been launched the only consequence would have been four times as many casualties. Neither Mametz Wood, the high ground on my right, nor Contalmaison, the height on my left, had fallen, nor indeed were they being seriously attacked and in such circumstances to attack the low ground between these heights was iniquitous folly. Two subsequent attacks were ordered by the corps with the same result.

Major-General T D Pilcher

When four or five days later Contalmaison and Mametz Wood were carried Quadrangle Support fell of itself.

If I had obeyed the corps more literally, I should have lost another two or three thousand men and have achieved no more. I was, as you know, accused of want of push, and consequently sent home. It is very easy to sit a few miles in the rear, and get credit for allowing men to be killed in an undertaking foredoomed to failure, but the part did not appeal to me and my protests against these useless attacks were not well received.'

Pilcher's service as commanding officer of the 17th Division is not recorded in the Army Lists.

Major-General I Phillips, by contrast to Major-General Pilcher, had more limited military experience and prior to the war had only attained the rank of Major before leaving the army and entering the world of politics. At the outbreak of war he was in the Pembrokeshire Yeomanry (Territorials) and had been Member of Parliament for Southampton for eight years and was very well connected too. He was a Liberal friend of David Lloyd George, the Chancellor of the Exchequer soon to become Prime Minister.

Even allowing for the passage of time and our opportunity to analyse the Great War in armchair contemplation it is not easy to understand why Phillips was so eager to put his comfortable existence to one side and seek to resurrect his army career. He was quickly promoted Brigadier-General in charge of the newly recruited 3 Brigade and within two months was again promoted this time to the Generalship of the Division, albeit with the suspicion of political tinkering. The urgency and fervour of the time and ignorance of what was to come may have had something to do with his decision making but he deserves credit, nevertheless, for coming forward when it would have been easy to stand back and let others take the lead. There must have been someone else more suitable even allowing for the shortage of officers.

Whatever his abilities as a general, however, he came into the war with the major liability of being a politician. Politics, as we know, can engender much division and as a Liberal he would have had enemies. Moreover he was prepared to operate politically and enjoyed direct contact with Lloyd George. This in turn would be threatening to his superiors, someone who could step outside the chain of command and according to one report was prepared to do so; for example, when the commanding officer of the 16th Royal Welsh Fusiliers was sent home by Phillips at the request of Lloyd George to become his Parliamentary Private Secretary. XV Corps apparently knew nothing of this until later. It is alleged that the 38th Division had a strong political atmosphere permeating through its command and there was considerable friction.

As far as his military prowess is concerned Phillips never had much opportunity to prove himself, nor for that matter to fail either. He merely acted as the 'go-between' passing orders from XV Corps to his brigades. Any variance to the orders was quickly spotted by XV Corps, as with the orders for the attack which was never launched and for which he was dismissed. His proposal to attack with a battalion was soon countermanded and replaced with a platoon.

He never seemed to have questioned XV Corps strategy as Pilcher did. However his order to his troops to fall back in the face of machine guns and await another bombardment, made from the background of recent civilian life, might have seemed realistic and sensible to him but would not have had the approval of his senior commanders.

There are other instances when much larger attacks failed to materialise, for example, the attack of the 1st Royal Welsh Fusiliers on Strip Trench, but the commander of the 7th Division who was responsible, Major-General Watts, was thought to be well suited to taking over from Major-General Phillips. It is more likely that as Phillips' appointment was political so his dismissal was similarly engineered.

Lieutenant-General Sir Henry Horne was born in 1861 and first commissioned with the Royal Artillery in 1880. Progress thereafter appears to have been slow and it was some twenty five years later that he achieved the rank of Lieutenant-Colonel. By 1910 he was a full colonel, thereafter his career moved on at considerable pace.

In May 1912 he was appointed Brigadier-General. Seventeen months later he was promoted to Major-General. Fifteen months later in January 1916 he was appointed Lieutenant-General in command of XV Corps. Although the events at the Quadrangle and Mametz Wood are not one of the better episodes of his career the overall view of the relative success in the south of the Somme battlefields of which he was a part probably resulted in his appointment as Commander of the First Army in August 1916 and he received a knighthood.

He was considered to be the foremost expert on artillery methods and innovation and is credited by some as having invented the creeping barrage.

After the war he retired and like Brigadier-General Evans started a family late in life before he died in 1929.

Brigadier-General H J Evans was born in 1861 the son of the Reverend T H Evans of Preston Capes, Northampton. On leaving Sandhurst he was gazetted into the King's Liverpool Regiment and saw active service on the North West Frontier and in South Africa.

In 1914 he was Colonel in Charge of the Army Records Office at Shrewsbury. He was promoted Brigadier General of 115 Brigade which he took to France. He had a lively mind and some of his ideas were seemingly ahead of his time having resemblance to commando methods. Like Pilcher, he too was frustrated by the obduracy of those above him and often expressed that frustration.

While he expected to be sent home after the failure of 7 July at Mametz Wood he was not dismissed in the same manner as Pilcher or Phillips and it was some six weeks later he was replaced. He retired to Penralley, Rhayader the home of his wife who subsequently gave birth to a son. He involved himself in local politics and youth work with the scouts. He is described as becoming sad and melancholy in later years feeling he had failed in the latter part of his career. Writing in 1958 his son stated that he always thought his father had been sacked but his later conclusion that he was discarded because of his age and challenging nature was supported by Wyn Griffith at that time. Evans died in February 1932.

**Brigadier-General
H J Evans**

EPILOGUE

BACK TO THE WOOD

Between 1916 and 1918 the war continued and the 38th Welsh Division was to distinguish itself during several engagements. One notable occasion was at the battle for Pilckem Ridge in 1917 when, alongside the Guards Division, it acquitted itself with distinction. By early 1918 on most fronts the Germans had been edged backwards yard by yard in a war of attrition that seemed to have no obvious end at an appalling cost in human life and suffering. In March the Germans struck out in one last massive offensive in an attempt to break through the allied defences and achieve victory. Initially they broke through pushing back the allies over the ground which they had so painfully won and in many places they were overrun.

On the battlefield of the Somme the troops found themselves retreating back through all the familiar places and even beyond with the Germans taking ground not previously held. The garrison town of Albert was evacuated by the British and surrounding villages, previously billets and rest areas fell into German possession. In Albert the legendary Golden Virgin hanging over the town fell, shelled by the British artillery situated on the ridge overlooking the town on the Amiens road.

The German advance slowed, lacking ammunition and supplies and with mounting casualties. The allies were able to regroup and re-organise and the 38th Welsh Division found themselves facing Aveluy Wood north of Albert with the 18th Division on their right and their old friends the 17th Northern Division on their left.

On 15 August patrols of the 38th Divisional troops pushed through Aveluy Wood and crossed the River Ancre and made contact with the enemy. Preparations were then made to cross the river which were completed by the 22 August when an attempt to make the crossing was hampered by the Germans who had prepared to defend their positions and make a strong counter attack. While clearing Aveluy Wood the British troops had to take great care in locating booby traps left by the Germans who also left messages for their pursuers. One amusing example found by the 17th Northern Divisional troops was written with limited knowledge of English and some misunderstanding of the term 'iron rations.'

My Dear Tommy,

Wenn are you coming. We are gone. Many pleasures in our cottages. Send not so many iron portions. Eat them your selfst.

Make Peace (word illegible) next time! Have you not enough?

Once through the German defences on the River Ancre rapid progress was achieved and the 24 August disposition of the 38th Division were as follows: on the right in contact with the 18th Division in front of La Boiselle was 113 Brigade. Facing Ovillers in the centre was 115 Brigade while way over on the left on the high ground south-east of Thiepval was 114 Brigade.

Once again the troops were able to push on with good progress on all fronts except at Ovillers where there was some resistance at the Lochnagar Crater before that area too was captured.

Meanwhile on 23 August, after a bombardment by the 18th Division the 7th Royal West Kents and the 8th Royal Berks cleared the town of Albert, flushing out pockets of resistance, smashing down barricades and defusing booby-traps. They were then relieved on the 24 August by the 7th Buffs and the 8th East Surreys who were able to push forward and by 2.30pm the 18th Divisional Artillery was established around Becourt Chateau and was turning its attention to positions in Mametz Wood and Caterpillar Valley.

Owing to the success of the 38th Division on the left the 8th East Surreys were also able to push forward north of Albert commencing the advance at 4.00am on 25 August. By 10.00am they reached positions in the Quadrangle facing the eastern side of the southern part of Mametz Wood. They were in touch with the 16th Royal Welsh Fusiliers on the left and the 7th Buffs on the right who had established positions forward of Bottom Wood and were in Cliff Trench. A further advance was impeded by machine gun and artillery fire, the machine guns appearing to be situated on the high ground in the region of Montauban Alley, Pommiers Redoubt and Danzig Alley.

In the early evening the 8th East Surreys moved into the valley along which the railway ran and at 7.00pm one company advanced across the remains of Wood Trench and Wood Support Trench to the eastern edge of Mametz Wood where they were once again held up by machine gun fire. At 8.00pm they were bombarded with gas and high explosive shells.

Meanwhile during the morning of the 25 August on the right of the 18th Division the 38th Division attacked Contalmaison and units of the 113th Brigade were through the village by the afternoon and the 16th Royal Welsh Fusiliers were looking down once more on Mametz

Wood, the scene of the 38th Divisions heroic exploits of over two years ago. Machine gun fire from the Montauban heights and from the right in Bazentin-le-Petit Wood held up progress.

Two companies of the 16th Royal Welsh Fusiliers advanced on the western edge of the wood at 5.00pm. One company pushed out patrols into the wood but found no opposition and occupied the eastern edge of the wood. The battalion followed and became very spread out in the wood but by 10.55pm the wood had been consolidated. The night was very dark and wet, many men lost direction and in the early hours of the 26 August much time was spent getting the battalion together and re-organising at Sabot Copse.

In the southern sector of the wood the 8th East Surreys were able to make good progress, again assisted by the swift advance of the men of the 38th Division. By 9.35am one company of the 8th East Surreys supported by four Vickers machine gun crews advanced through Mametz Wood meeting no opposition and continuing east of Mametz Wood in touch with the 16th Royal Welsh Fusiliers on their left. They got forward into Marlborough Copse with their machine guns and were able to bring exceptionally effective enfilade fire on to Caterpillar Wood and on to the German machine gunners holding out in there. Montauban village was also attacked in the same way and thus enabled the 7th Buffs to advance forward of White Trench creeping behind the British barrage in small mobile independent groups known as 'fire and movement' tactics which had replaced the old wave formation and by 4.30pm Montauban was captured.

At 4.00am on the 26 August an attack was launched on Bazentin-le-Grand. The 13th Royal Welsh Fusiliers led the attack with the 16th Royal Welsh Fusiliers and the 14th Royal Welsh Fusiliers in the rear on the right and left respectively.

The battalions formed up in Death Valley near the site where the German machine gunners had caused such destruction to their colleagues in the 38th Division on 7 July 1916 and moved off. Once again the German machine gunners were active from their position in Caterpillar Wood by some irony the same positions which the Welsh gunners had occupied on that fateful day and the 16th Royal Welsh Fusiliers and 14th Royal Welsh Fusiliers were held up for some time.

Later that day Bazentin-le-Grand fell and the German machine gunners were silenced for the last time in Caterpillar Wood and the war moved on from the environs of Mametz Wood for the last time.

THE DRAGON RETURNS

In the nineteen-eighties on a visit to the Somme Battlefields Sergeant Tom Price, a veteran of the Battle of Mametz Wood, was surprised to find that there was no memorial to the 38th Division at the scene of their great sacrifice and returned to Wales determined to do something about it.

The Western Front Association is pledged to keep alive the memory and sacrifices made in the Great War and has many branches nation-wide. In 1985 a sub-committee of the South Wales Branch was appointed under the chairmanship of Mr H W Evans. The target was to raise £20,000 and fund raising commenced in earnest. A radio broadcast early in 1986 made by BBC Wales but also heard in many other regions provided a vital breakthrough. Telling the story of the Battle for Mametz Wood and of the proposals to create a memorial it was the stimulus for many to send in their donations.

The notable sculptor David Petersen of St Clears, Carmarthenshire, was commissioned to create the memorial, a Welsh Dragon. David Petersen proposed that the sculpture should not glorify war but speak of courage and gallantry and hopefully comment on the futility of war. There were, though, many problems in the history of its construction.

The first choice of material for the plinth was to be of Welsh slate, but this proved to be too expensive and Forest of Dean stone was finally chosen. The chalk ground on which the memorial was to stand was not stable enough to support the weight of nine tonnes and so a concrete inverted pyramid was sunk under the base stones to support the structure. Cost factors also limited the choice of material to steel rather than bronze and the Dragon was hand forged in David Petersen's studios. When completed the Dragon was taken over to France in April 1987 by the 157 (TA) Royal Corps of Transport, based in Cardiff, who had also taken the stone blocks for the plinth the previous month. David Petersen travelled to France to supervise the fixing of the sculpture to the plinth by a local firm of builders.

The Dragon is shown head slightly to one side, looking out at the Hammerhead, tearing up a single strand of barbed wire. The barbed wire represents the war and its breaking the end of war and repression. The cap badges of the three Welsh Regiments are cut into the stone plinth.

On the 71st Anniversary of the Capture of the Wood the Memorial Dragon was dedicated. It bears the inscription *Parchwn eu hymdrechion parhaed ein hatgofion* (We revere their endeavours. May

Sculptor David Petersen about to instal the Dragon.

Brigadier Anthony Vivian with Private Gwynoro Morris at the dedication of the Red Dragon Memorial in July 1987.

Albert Evans wounded at Mametz Wood.

Tom Price (left) with fellow veteran Bill Parry Morris MM at Flat Iron Copse Cemetery in 1985.

we continue to remember). Welsh voices were again raised and echoed across Death Valley as they had done all those years ago. The surviving veterans who made the journey with their relatives and friends led the wreath laying and the Last Post was sounded by two buglers of the Royal Welsh Fusiliers supported by a French Army Garde D'Honneur. Music was provided by the band of the 1st Battalion of the Royal Regiment of Wales who marched impressively led by Taffy the goat mascot. The Kilgetty Male Voice Choir led the singing.

One absent friend was Tom Price, from whom the whole idea originated, sadly he did not live to take part in an emotional day. No doubt he was there, somewhere, among all the rest of the Welsh boys and their brothers from further afield, who, many are convinced still haunt the depths of Mametz Wood.

George Richards was the first veteran to lay a wreath at the dedication of the Red Dragon Memorial. He was accompanied by Mr R Price, son of Tom Price.

Later the Brigadier commanding the current 160th Infantry brigade went to speak to the veterans. George was not impressed.

'What lot are you with then son?' he asked.

George had known some officers in the Great War and he had told them a thing or two from time to time.

'I'm sure they were glad of your advice' replied the General.

That day at Mametz Wood was not for brigadiers it was for 'the boys', the privates and the lance-corporals and George knew it.

Inauguration of the 38th (Welsh) Division Memorial with buglers of the Royal Welch Fusiliers in July 1987.

Mametz veteran George Richards.

VISITING THE BATTLEFIELDS

The quickest route to the Somme is to cross from Dover to Calais (or Folkestone to Calais via the Shuttle). From Calais follow the sign A26 Arras and Paris. The Autoroute will be quiet. Continue to the junction of the A26/A1 continuing to follow the signs to Paris. As you join the A1 the traffic will be heavier but the journey is only a short one to exit 16 for Bapaume. The distance from Calais is about 90 miles. From Bapaume take the D929 to Albert.

You should book your accommodation in advance. The growth in numbers of those visiting the battlefields has been reflected in an increase in available accommodation. An imbalance, though, still exists. Remember the area is rural and agricultural, the nearest large hotels are in Amiens or Arras.

If you have nowhere to stay call at the Office du Tourisme in Albert. This is opposite the Basilique (Cathedral). The staff at the Office du Tourisme speak English. I have included a selective list of accommodation as an appendix to this section to assist the reader to make an advance booking.

What you need to have in your luggage will depend on what time of year you decide to visit. Winter can be colder on the Somme and wetter too! Full waterproofs together with wellingtons are essential. Warm clothing should include gloves and headwear. A day sack is also useful to put in your camera, small first aid kit, penknife, bottle opener, corkscrew and refreshments and books, maps and pens. Summer can still present wet conditions even though the average rainfall is less than in Britain. It can also be considerably hotter in summer and temperatures can soar above 30°C or more. Protection in the form of headwear and sun cream is essential. Always have available plenty to drink, not necessarily alcohol for that can be counterproductive in more ways than one.

Driving in the Somme should present few problems. The roads with a few exceptions are much quieter and in this area you are as likely to meet a British registered car as a French one. There are however some important differences to remember and the first and most important one is to remember to drive on the right. The most dangerous time is when first setting out after a halt. It is very easy to pull out on to the left of the carriageway with potentially disastrous results.

The cheapness and availability of alcohol together with the distance from home should not lure the visitor into believing it is all right to drink and drive. The alcohol limit is lower than at home in Britain (50 milligrams) and it is rigorously enforced by regular road blocks for mass on the spot testing and there is no escape!

It is also a legal requirement to carry a warning triangle and a set of replacement light bulbs. All documents should be carried too, this includes, insurance, driving licence and registration document. Your insurance should include a 'Green Card' for full European Cover, obtainable through your insurance company. Breakdown insurance is a matter for your own judgement. There are several garages in Albert who act as agents for most popular makes of cars and I know several instances of their services being well received.

The final point on motoring is to beware of the rule 'Priority from the Right'. In all cases unless marked otherwise you must give way to the traffic approaching anywhere from the right. This includes traffic approaching you ostensibly from ahead but offset to the right. The sign to look for is a cross X which indicates priority from the right at the next junction.

As a member of the EEC Britain has a reciprocal arrangement with France and other European member countries for obtaining medical treatment. By obtaining forms E111 from any Post Office you will be able to take advantage of this but in the case of France this falls well short of what you expect at home. In the first place you may be asked for money 'up front'. Treatment and any drugs must be paid for and then claimed back in the same way that a French national is required to do from the local social security office. Only a proportion of the costs will be refunded — between 60% and 80%. Medical treatment can be expensive and the claimant could still be presented with a substantial bill. It should also be remembered that such things as re-arranged hotel and travel expenses or repatriation are not covered. No special inoculations are necessary but it is advisable to have tetanus injections. The Somme is a high risk area, because of its history, all agricultural workers are obliged to have injections. There are many agencies offering travel insurance – a few pounds for a few days would seem a reasonable risk investment. There are also now annual policies which are good value for money which offer an unlimited number of trips.

Always have your passport with you. The French have a national identity card and the Gendarmes and Police could ask you to provide proof of identity. The Somme region is a quiet and on the whole a trouble free area but crime does exist. Be careful not to leave valuables in your car. There have been instances of British cars being broken in to while the owners were away walking or visiting a distant cemetery.

Albert is the largest centre of population, most of the soldiers involved in the fighting on the Somme would be familiar with it. It was a garrison town just behind the British lines and was regularly shelled by German artillery. Its most famous landmark is the Madonna and Child on top of the Basilque which hung precariously over for most of the duration of the war. It was said at the time that when it fell the war would end. Many years later a veteran friend of mine, Alan Walmsley of the Duke of Wellingtons Regiment, was always sceptical about the legend of the Golden Virgin. With his dry northern sense of humour he said 'That couldn't be right, you know, 'cos the bloody Royal Engineers wired it up!'. Today it stands above the town and shines out at night, a beacon which can be seen from many points across the surrounding countryside. The floodlighting was renewed in 1996 as part of the Commemoration of the 80th Anniversary of the Battle of the Somme. It is Albert in which most visitors find most convenient to do their shopping and buy fuel. There is an interesting underground museum dedicated to the First World War. It is housed in tunnels used as shelters during the Second World War and the entrance is signposted near the west end of the Basilique.

Alan Walmsley

Finally, the visitor to the Somme will almost certainly come across the debris of war. Although recently there have been renewed efforts to clear up live shells, hand grenades and mortar bombs as they come to light, there are still many of these potentially lethal objects about. It is as well to remember that the cemeteries we visit and memorials we look at represent tens of thousands killed by these explosives.

The Golden Virgin in 1916 and (right) in 1996.

WHERE TO STAY

Listed Hotels in Albert

***   Royal Picardie, Route d'Amiens 80300
       Tel (0033)322753700   Fax (0033)322756019

**   La Basilique, 3 Rue Gambetta 80300
       Tel (0033)322750471   Fax (0033)322751047

*   Hotel de la Paix, 39 Rue Victor Hugo 80300
       Tel (0033)322750164   Fax (0033)322754417

Listed Chambres d'Hotes (Bed & Breakfast)

***   Nr Beaumont Hamel
       Les Galets, Route de Beaumont, Auchonvilliers 80560
       Tel (0033)322762879   Fax (0033)322762879

***   Ginchy, 1 Grande Rue 80360
       Tel (0033)322850224   Fax (0033)322851160

***   Grandcourt, 9 Rue de Beaucourt 80300
       Tel (0033)322748158   Fax (0033)322748168

***   Mailly-Maillet, 27 Rue de P. Lefevre 80560
       Tel (0033)322762144

Other Recommended Establishments

There are few facilities in the battlefield area itself for the tourist. However those looking for refreshment or somewhere to have a meal will find the following satisfactory:

Authuille

    Auberge de la Valleé d'Ancre
A good quality restaurant at reasonable prices
6 Rue Moulin, 80300
Tel 0322751518

Ovillers

Le Poppy
A cheap but good 'Les Routiers' style restaurant
4 Route Bapaume, 80300
Tel 0322754545

Auchonvilliers

Avril Williams Guest House
A warm welcome assured, lunches, table licence, bed and breakfast
10 Rue Delattre, 80560
Tel (0033)322762366

WALKING AND TOURING

It is possible to visit and view much of the area described in the foregoing narrative and this will be easily recognisable as the ground has changed little over the intervening years. The shape of some of the woodland has altered in places but for the most part this very attractive corner of the battlefields has changed little and provides the visitor with the opportunity to walk its sheltered, secluded, little valleys and with it comes a feeling of solitude and remoteness. It is a haven for wildlife. Buzzards often soar above the tree tops while harriers skim the ridges and woodpeckers are both seen and heard. Hares and rabbits scurry about and it is not unusual to see deer bounding from Caterpillar Wood or Bottom Wood into the greater security of Mametz Wood.

It is imperative though, to remember that all the ground belongs to someone and to respect it. Generations of French farmers have indulged the visitors to their fields and with a few exceptions it is possible to walk on ploughed fields or the stubble after the harvest without hindrance. However, on no account should crops be walked on and the instances of this occurring are unfortunately on the increase. Likewise, so is antipathy from the farming community which is not surprising when, as happened recently, a well known tour company, spilled a whole coach load on to the side of the road and then made off straight across the growing crops!

The woods, too, are private and should only be entered with permission, a gamekeeper (Gard du Chasse) or woodman may be on hand and might authorise a stroll if approached but visitations by those armed with metal detectors have put them on their guard and such requests may be declined. Beware, during the shooting season from the end of September to the end of February. The French are fanatical hunters and tend to shoot anything that moves, even each other on occasions!

This section has been designed with those in mind who wish, or who may only able to walk short distances but it also caters for those with greater ambition in as much that the routes, with one exception, dovetail, thus allowing an extended expedition to be undertaken.

The driving tour covers some parts of the walking routes and should be undertaken with this in mind as where these coincide the fuller description will be given in the walking route.

DRIVING TOUR

Leave Albert on the D938 travelling towards Peronne and pass

149

Fricourt on the left. Also pass the major left turn signposted for both Fricourt and Mametz and continue until a square brick building appears on your left. Turn left here. This is the site of the railway halt where the 1st Royal Welsh Fusiliers and 2nd Royal Irish convened for their attacks on Mametz Wood. The railway, rebuilt after the war, has now gone but the halt remains, recently inhabited, but now a store complete with station nameplate 'Mametz' and 'Gare'.

Take the road from Mametz to Fricourt. As Fricourt is entered the road reaches the site of Rose Cottage on the right of a junction and as described in the walking route. Take the road on the right signposted to the German Cemetery. Follow the route as described in Walk 4. It is permissible to drive down the side of Fricourt Wood towards the farm and likewise to turn left at the farm and thence back onto the metalled road. Turn left to the German Cemetery. After leaving the German Cemetery turn the car around and drive towards Contalmaison passing the eastern end of Shelter Wood from where on the right excellent views of the Hedge Line and further on Bottom Wood can be obtained. The small copse is the Quadrangle and beyond that the western side of Mametz Wood can also be seen.

Further down the road as Peake Wood Cemetery is passed a track will be observed under the fold of the hill on the right. The western end of Quadrangle Trench curved round above the track keeping to the higher contours. Somewhere near the end of the track Shelter Alley ran up the escarpment and joined Quadrangle Trench. Note the shell scarring still visible in the fields on the right. As Contalmaison is entered look for a small concealed turning on the right to Mametz. This sign is not visible from the direction you have come. Follow the road to the communal cemetery and read the appropriate section in Walk 5. Continue down the road but first set the trip on your car's speedometer to nought. When you have travelled four tenths of a mile you will be within a few yards of the place where Quadrangle Trench crossed the road. About thirty metres in the field on your left was the junction of Quadrangle Trench with Quadrangle Alley which led to the German 'block'. On the right in the field about 120 metres distant Bottom Alley ran from Quadrangle Trench towards Bottom Wood.

Views of the Hedge Line and Bottom Wood can be seen on the right. Quadrangle Wood or Copse is straight ahead while Dantzig Alley Cemetery can be seen on the horizon.

Mametz Wood is on the left and more or less parallel with the end of the strip of trees in the valley, Wood Trench ran back to the western edge of Mametz Wood. Strip Trench ran down the edge of the wood.

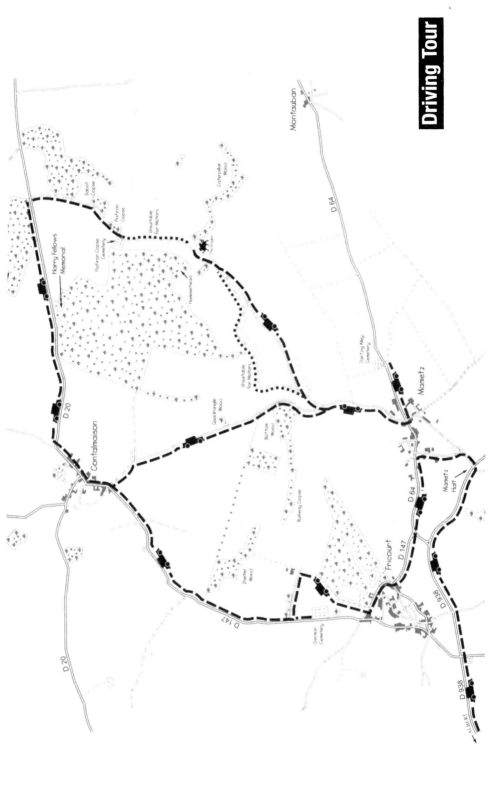

Montauban

D 64

Darling Alley Cemetery

Mametz

Caterpillar Wood

The Sunkeni

Hammerhead

Unsuitable for Motors

Flatiron Copse Cemetery

Flatiron Copse

Sabot Copse

Harry Fellows Memorial

D 20

Contalmaison

Quadrangle Wood

Unsuitable for Motors

Bottom Wood

Railway Copse

Mametz Halt

D 64

Fricourt

D 147

Shelter Wood

D 20

German Cemetery

D 147

D 938

ALBERT

D 938

Looking down the road from Contalmaison Cemetery towards Quadrangle Wood. Repeated German attacks from the right (Quadrangle Trench) failed to dislodge the defenders of Quadrangle Support Trench located in the field to the left.

The memorial seat at the Dragon was placed there by Major Huw Rodge in memory of his father (above) who fought at Mamtez Wood. When his father returned he found that his family had sold all his belongings believing him to be dead and he promptly left home. He revisted the Somme only once when a farmer attempted to charge him sixpence for crossing his field – he never returned.

Continue down the road until a track is reached on the right. It is a short stroll up to the front of Bottom Wood and the Hedge Line beyond. There appears to be no trace of Bottom Alley where it extended into the wood, but beyond in the Hedge Line what seems to be distinct traces of the old trench can be seen in places. There are excellent views of the ground in front of Quadrangle Trench. Return to the car and note on the far left regular deep indentations in the bank on the left, the origins of which I have found no reliable explanation for. Some have had trees planted in them. Turn sharp left following the sign to the Memorial and take the lower road and follow the information given in Walk 3. It should be possible to drive along the lower road in all but the wettest of conditions. (If in doubt turn round and take the top road). In due course you will meet the junction of the top road and continue to the Welsh Memorial Dragon.

It is about 500 yards further on to Flat Iron Copse Cemetery and if you consider that it is possible to negotiate the first fifty yards of the track you should have no problem with the remainder. Otherwise you will have to approach it from Bazentin le Petit via the metalled road, or walk it from where you are parked.

Return to Mametz village using the top road which roughly follows the site of White Trench, Cliff Trench turned off to the right. Pass the entrance to Queen's Nullah on the left. On the right there are views of the

152

front of Fricourt Wood and in the near foreground Railway Alley came across the field and entered the wood about 200 yards from the road. Enter the village by the war memorial on the left, turn left and drive the short distance to Dantzig Alley Cemetery. Refer to the second part of Walk 3, Part 2.

To visit Marlborough Copse follow the road from Dantzig Alley Cemetery passing the site of Pommiers Redoubt to Montauban. In the village turn left and drive through the small streets bearing to the left and to the single track road that leads directly to the Copse and Caterpillar Wood. See the text of Walk 1 for information. Return to the village and follow the signposts to the village of Longueval. Here take the road to Contalmaison. After passing Bazentin on the right a sign will be seen indicating a left turn to Flat Iron Copse Cemetery.

WALK 1 - THE ATTACK OF 7 JULY MAMETZ WOOD
Duration about one hour

Starting from the Dragon Memorial it should be possible to cross the narrow field to the Hammerhead opposite. At the time of writing there has been for some years, a large tract of 'set-a-side' land that is not used for cultivation. If this disappears in the future, then as long as there are no crops in the field there should be no objection to walking across anyway. Failing this to the right of the memorial there is a dividing strip between two fields which should enable access to be gained. Keep to the edge of the field, remember that the wood should not be entered unless permission has been obtained and follow the edge of the wood northwards. Looking to the left you will see excellent views right to left of Caterpillar Wood, the valley and the ridge, all the ground, in fact, across which the 16th Welsh on the left and the 11th South Wales Borderers on the right attacked. As they came over the ridge it is easy to imagine the German machine gunners in position on the edge of the wood where the reader is standing taking every advantage of the exposed troops in front of them. The attack was delivered on a frontage of about 500 yards. It is about 700 yards from the Dragon to Flat Iron Copse Cemetery ahead. It will be appreciated how close, therefore, the right flank of the 16th Welsh was to the machine gunners in Flat Iron and Sabot Copses which were linked to the German second position.

Flat Iron Copse cemetery was started after the capture of Mametz Wood and is notable for the existence of the graves of three sets of brothers who are buried there. Both the brothers Tregaskis and Hardwidge have a mention elsewhere in this book. Private Ernest

E Dwyer VC

Flat Iron Copse Cemetery.

Philby and Private Herbert Philby of the Middlesex Regiment died on 21 August 1916 when their battalion was attacked by gas shells.

Also buried in this cemetery is Corporal E Dwyer who won the Victoria Cross near Ypres in Belgium in April 1915. Prior to being killed in September near Guillemont a few miles from here he had taken part in recruiting campaigns talking about and recording his experiences. An example of this still exists and has been reissued as part of a Great War compilation by Pavilion Records.

Return towards the Dragon. At the time of writing the fields on the left above the bank have had a large tract of 'set-a-side' for some time and it is possible to walk back along the top of the bank if preferred, from where better views are obtained.

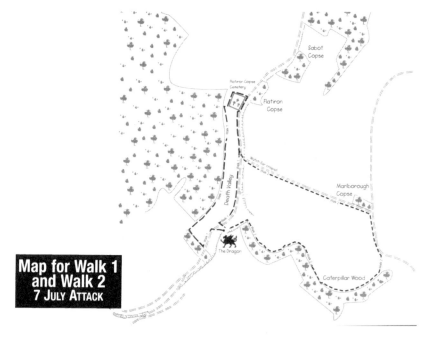

Map for Walk 1 and Walk 2
7 JULY ATTACK

WALK 2
Duration about 1 hour

About two thirds of the way back there is a track running to the left. Although shown on the French equivalent of our ordnance survey maps as extending to the bottom of the field the farmer has ploughed about the last 100 yards up and it may not be possible to reach it at certain times of the year without going over crops. If it is possible to get on to the track this will go directly to Marlborough Copse and to the areas where the attacking battalions of the 38th Division gathered prior to forming up behind the crest of the ridge on 7 July. Turning round and looking back will give exceptional views of the Hammerhead and other parts of Mametz Wood to the south.

The village in front is Montauban and it is possible to return to the Dragon by following the edge of Caterpillar Wood along which there is yet another long standing stretch of 'set-a-side' along the whole route, emerging at the end of the valley where the left flank of the 11th South Wales Borderers advanced.

If it is not possible to access the track as described above then the alternative route to Marlborough Copse would be to walk up the edge of Caterpillar Wood, returning the same way.

At the end of Caterpillar Wood turn left into some rough ground with long grass, pass through the remains of an old barbed wire fence and turn right downhill towards the memorial car park. You should pass the remains of a concrete bunker of which only part of the roof is now visible before reaching your starting point again.

WALK 3 – ATTACK OF 10 JULY – MAMETZ WOOD

Approach on the signposted road to the Welsh memorial from Mametz village to where the single track road forks; take the lower left hand track and continue until it turns sharp right at about 400 yards.

It should be possible to park a vehicle by the hunters' lodge on the corner.

Walk on about fifty yards until the point where the end of the narrow part of Mametz Wood approaches the track. Cross the rough ground and look to the left. There are clearly discernible traces of a trench which if followed become deeper and end in a series of large shell holes which destroyed the trench at that point. It is possible that this is the remains of the trench dug to connect Strip Trench with Cliff Trench. Cliff Trench was situated on the ridge just behind the hunters' lodge. Walk to the right of the wood, keeping to the edge of the wood. There are plenty of opportunities to see the remains of Strip Trench on the left as the wood is very narrow before it broadens out. This is the part of the wood attacked initially by the 16th Royal Welsh Fusiliers. Further on there is a gap in the wood through which a natural gas pipeline has been laid. Just beyond this point is the approximate point where Lieutenant-Colonel Carden was killed on the edge of the wood. Look to the right and you will see a pronounced hollow in the ground in front of the track. If the ground is ploughed you will also see a dark strip of ground stretching across the field. This is the site of the railway track and where Captain Glynn Jones regrouped the 14th Royal Welsh Fusiliers.

Continue along the edge of the wood, on the left vestiges of trenches and defences can still be seen just inside the wood. Facing the wood is the ridge down which the attacking battalions of the 38th Division approached. Just before an old wire fence and some bushes are reached the entrance to the central ride of the wood will be found. It was from here that the Germans emerged with a white flag and surrendered to Captain Glynn Jones.

Continue along the edge of the wood and good distant views of Marlborough Copse and the Dragon can be seen. As the southern edge of the Hammerhead comes closer you are now approaching the approximate position attacked by Lieutenant Cowie and his platoon when he silenced a German machine gun before losing his life. It is not possible to be certain of the exact position.

As the Hammerhead is reached, in the corner, the first crossride will be found, which was the first objective on the 10 July. It is possible to see it disappearing to the opposite side of the wood. This was the site of much confusion and the position from where the troops outran the British barrage and had to retire because of inflexibility in the artillery plans.

Turn right and follow the southern edge of the Hammerhead. There is a small clearing on the left which forms the 'head' of the hammer on the map. In 1916 it was a much bigger area and it was here that Lieutenant J Evans and two platoons of men held on when counter attacked by the Germans through the wood and for which Evans was awarded the Military Cross. It should be possible to return from the wood to the track across long standing 'set-a-side' but should this disappear then there is a track to the right near the trees. Follow this and turn right keeping to the lower track where it divides following it below the ridge. The long rising approach ground crossed by the attacking troops on 10 July can be appreciated before arriving at the quarry. Much earth moving in recent years has uncovered the remains

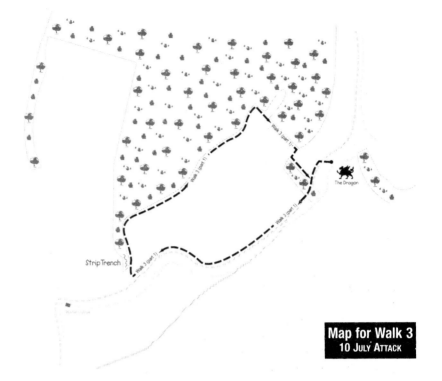

Strip Trench

Walk 3 (part 1)

Walk 3 (part 1)

Walk 3 (part 1)

The Dragon

Map for Walk 3
10 July Attack

of several German dugouts and a large quantity of corrugated metal is lying around together with several live shells. All along the banking on the left were numerous dugouts made initially by the Germans and extended later by the British as the valley became a supply route. Evidence can also be seen of the bombardment it received with many shell holes clearly visible. As the valley was cleared at the end of the war it was reported that much debris was thrown into the bank and it was littered with battered equipment, including old helmets and rifles.

Even now it is possible to scramble up the bank and find old tins, bottles and shell fragments barely covered by the fallen pine needles, especially in the winter period. While preparing this walk the author found several live shells, two grenades, a rather battered Tommy's

The Dragon viewed from the edge of the wood, the 'Hammerhead' on the left and Marlborough copse on the horizon.

helmet, part of a bicycle, a screw picket for holding barbed wire and bolts and fishplates from the old railway track.

You will now be back at your starting point.

Unfortunately it is difficult to get an extensive view of the area from the bank above, but there is a gap in the trees that does give some view of Strip Trench and beyond. It is possible to visit the site of Strip Trench, Wood Trench and Wood Support Trench by walking up the left hand side of the wood. The wood is very narrow here where it comes towards the track like a pointing finger. Strip Trench is clearly identifiable even after all the shelling it received and the subsequent passage of time, just inside the edge of the wood. When approximately 450 yards have been covered you will have reached the site of Wood Trench which turned at right angles out of the wood to form the major defensive position. Thereafter Strip Trench continued, more of a communication trench, a further 450 yards approximately until it reached Wood Support Trench. About fifty yards from the corner of the wood it is still possible to see Wood Support Trench emerging from the wood at this point about three feet in depth. Looking west it is possible to appreciate how easy it was to enfilade the advance of the 38th Division through the wood from the position in the Quadrangle.

From this point it is possible to continue your walk around the edge of the wood taking in Walk 5, making a circular walk by returning from Contalmaison Cemetery via the road which passes Quadrangle Wood.

WALK 3 PART 2
QUEEN'S NULLAH - DANTZIG ALLEY CEMETERY
Waking time 1 hour

The starting point is the same as Walk 3. The track where you are standing is the same track on which the 2nd Royal Irish found themselves halted while a patrol went into Strip Trench on the night of 4 July and found German soldiers nearby. Walk back towards Mametz village along the track. The bank on the right is where the 2nd Royal Irish took the breech blocks from the guns. As you approach the junction where the upper track on the left rejoins the lower track a large rubbish dump will be seen. I have searched for the possible site of the quarry where the 1st Royal Welsh Fusiliers took shelter after having got lost. This is the most likely site as for very many years there was a large rubbish dump on the corner here which about four years ago became full up. A further dump was made by digging out another artificial 'quarry' which at the same time exposed some tunnels of a German dugout in the chalk. Subsequent erosion has now eliminated all traces of this position.

Just after the junction a small track will be seen on the left. This is the entrance to Queen's Nullah. It will be remembered that this was the scene of multifarious activity and of various battalion and brigade headquarters and of an advanced dressing station. The quarry appears to be recent. A track leads from Queen's Nullah direct to Dantzig Alley Cemetery. Danzig Alley Trench (note the different spelling) ran along the opposite side of the road. All the original burials are in Plot 1 but after the end of the war eight other cemeteries were concentrated into Dantzig Alley.

In addition to the graves of those specifically mentioned in the text of the book other graves of men from both the 17th Division and 38th Division can be found here.

At the back of the cemetery there are excellent long distance views across the Quadrangle and Mametz Wood. A memorial seat will also be found dedicated to the 14th Royal Welsh Fusiliers. A translation of the inscription in Welsh reads:

> ***Distance cannot make you forgotten***
> ***The Children of thou dear hills***
> ***Heart and heart remain together***
> ***Even when separated***

Map for Walk 3 (Part 2) Dantzig Alley

These are the words of Private E H Evans, 15th Royal Welsh Fusiliers, killed in action 31 July 1917. An award winning film was made in recent years telling how at the moment of achieving his ambition of being awarded the Bardic Chair at Birkenhead in 1917 he had been killed, never to know of his achievement. The chair was draped in black instead. The film is called *Hedd Wynn* which was Ellis Evan's bardic name. He is buried at Artillery Wood Cemetery, Boesinghe, Belgium.

The site of Pommiers Redoubt is further up the

159

Dantzig Alley Cemetery with The Royal Welsh Fusiliers Memorial Seat.

road to the right towards Montauban. It is about 350 yards walk but there is nothing to be seen of this well known spot which was situated on the right hand side of the road and took its name from the apple trees that grew in the vicinity at the time. To return, it is possible to retrace your steps or go back through the village. If you wish to visit the church, where there is a memorial to the 38th Welsh Division, call at the first house on the right as you enter the village and obtain the key.

Turn right at the crossroads and note the village war memorial on the corner with the shell cases. Follow the road back past the entrance to Queen's Nullah and the hunters' lodge.

WALK 4
FRICOURT - RAILWAY ALLEY- SHELTER WOOD

Approaching Fricourt on the D938 from Albert take the first turning left signposted into the village, pass the British Cemetery on the left and park conveniently near the Salle de Fête (Village Hall) in the Rue d'Ipswich. Opposite, on the left hand side of the road leading to Contalmaison. There is a track between some farm buildings and a white walled house numbered eleven. Follow the track until some rough ground is reached on the right. This is part of the Triple Tambour Mine Craters on the old German front line. Part of it is fenced off with cattle but it is normally possible to look over this part although it is very overgrown. The ground in front was that over which the British attacked on both the 1 and 2 July. The cemetery in front, Fricourt New Military Cemetery has over 200 burials mostly those of the 10th West Yorkshires (17th Division) who suffered the highest casualties of any battalion on 1 July. On 2 July, on your left the 6th Lincoln's attacked and likewise on the right, the 8th South Staffordshires went forward.

Returning to where you parked the car take the road to the right signposted Mametz and named Rue du Marshal Foch until you reach a sign for the German Military Cemetery to the left. This is the site of Rose Cottage where the 6th Lincolns were held up. A track leads straight ahead along the edge of the wood. This was the site of

Sunshine Alley Trench. Follow the road to the left and Fricourt Chateau will be found on the right, where several brigades had their headquarters in the cellars. Continue to the water tower and then right up the side of Fricourt Wood. The ground on the left was covered by the 8th South Staffordshires while the 6th Lincolns pushed through the wood. Continue walking until Fricourt Farm is reached on the left. Here, on the right, good views of the front of Fricourt Wood can be seen and across the middle of the fields in front was the site of Railway Alley. Railway Copse can be seen but it is generally more wooded around the area now than it was in 1916.

Straight ahead and beyond the Crucifix was the Poodles, originally two trees, but no longer there. Walking on Shelter Wood will be reached where a battalion of the 186th German Regiment surrendered. The path finishes at the eastern edge of Shelter Wood but good views of the ground ahead up to the Hedge Line and Bottom Wood can be obtained. Note the shell damaged field on the right where the railway line ran.

Return to Fricourt Farm which is built on the site of Lozenge Trench. The original Farm was on the other side of the track in 1916. Turn right and walk towards the road, on the left is the remains of Lozenge Wood in which it is possible to find the remains of Lozenge Trench. Turn left towards the centre of the village. The German Cemetery will be seen on the left which contains the remains of over 17,000 German soldiers, mostly in mass graves. Lonely Copse is passed just after leaving the cemetery on the left. Continue back to the *Salle de Fête*. Fricourt church contains a plaque dedicated to the memory of the men of the 17th Northern Division who died in the Great War, 494 officers and 8,421 other ranks. Major R G Raper who commanded the 8th South Staffordshires in this attack on 2 July is also commemorated in the church which is not always open. Enquiries should be made at the school.

Fricourt Chateau where several brigades had their headquarters in the cellars. Above is as it was in 1914 and below a comparison taken in the 1990s.

Remains of German strong point and a fortified well in front of Fricourt Wood built on for present-day use.

Major Raper was originally buried in a separate private grave and so became regarded as the liberator of Fricourt. The villagers named the road after him that leads from the church to the village war memorial. He is now interred in Fricourt British Cemetery (Bray Road) near where your walk has finished.

WALK 5
WOOD SUPPORT TRENCH/QUADRANGLE ALLEY

This walk starts at the Communal Cemetery at Contalmaison which can be found on the road (C5) to Mametz. There are excellent views of the Quadrangle area and the western approaches of Mametz Wood. At the rear of the civilian cemetery is the memorial to the 12th Battalion of the Manchester Regiment, who, it will be recalled, lost so heavily in their attack on Quadrangle Support Trench on 7 July. It commemorates all those of the battalion who fell in the Great War.

The point where the track at the side of the cemetery meets the road was on the line of Pearl Alley. Stand looking directly down the C5 towards Mametz. On your immediate right the attackers attempted to get forward up Pearl Alley towards the junction with Quadrangle Support Trench.

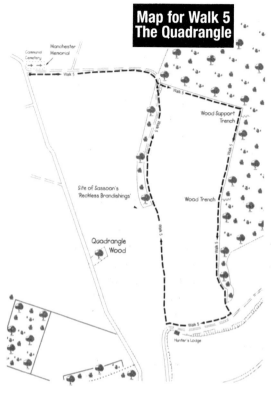

Walk down the track by the side of the cemetery, after about 150 yards you will come to the site of Quadrangle Support Trench which ran parallel to the metalled road for about 350 yards. On the left, about fifty yards into the field is the site of the junction between Pearl Alley and Quadrangle Support Trench. It is in this area that Lieutenant Stanbury was wounded and last seen. A further 100 yards on the left the site of Acid Drop Copse will be seen from where deadly machine gun fire could fire directly down the valley in a southerly direction. It is also possible here to see how Quadrangle Support Trench lay over the crest of a spur and was not only invisible until attacking troops were on to it but was also extremely difficult to get artillery observation on to. Artillery fire for the most part fell very short. The result was that the Germans holding the trench had not suffered when the infantry advanced. Lieutenant-Colonel Castle of the 17th Division Royal Field Artillery was at the time attached to the 24th Division and was in Railway Alley. He could see the attacks being made and could even see Germans bringing up their machine guns on their shoulders as each fruitless attack was made. Some field guns of a neighbouring division stood nearby but he was refused permission to make use of them, controlling their fire by direct vision. The timetable of the artillery barrage did not allow for any flexibility.

It will be appreciated how Quadrangle Support Trench looked down on a bare natural glacis without a scrap of cover except, perhaps, for the inevitable shell holes.

Continue walking down the track until the wood is reached. This part of the wood is now known as Contalmaison Wood and it was about twenty yards inside the wood where Captain Job was killed. Follow the track to the top side of the line of trees and in about 100 yards you will arrive at the western end of Wood Support. This is where Second-Lieutenant Clarke and later Lieutenant Davidson of the 6th Dorsets were mortally wounded attacking the strong point. Continue along the track which suddenly ends, but it should be possible to walk along the edge of the field and reach the end of the line of trees. Fifty yards to your left was the end of Wood Trench captured by the Dorsets. Look to the right across the little valley through which the railway ran. On the far side, about 100 yards from the valley bottom just below the highest contour of the ground was the western end of Quadrangle Trench. It was across this valley that Lieutenant Sassoon made his dash to 'capture' Wood Trench after the death of Lance-Corporal Kendall who was sniped on the opposite bank.

Go through the trees, there is a gap and also a convenient long standing piece of 'set-a-side' which enables access to be gained on to the site of Quadrangle Trench. It is also possible to walk along the top of the contour about 250 yards and reach the approximate site of the 'block' in Quadrangle Alley. This is the scene of Lieutenant Holroyd's attempt to get to the junction on the 7 July and later on 10 July Second-Lieutenant Goodwin was repulsed by machine gun fire while attempting to move forward up the valley.

It was also here that both Lieutenant Cracroft and Captain Heathcock lost their lives in the final attempt to break through made by the 7th East Yorkshires.

All this could eventually change of course if the ground is ploughed up and planted, nevertheless the area is a fine vantage point, quite remote and an excellent place to read the account of the struggle where it happened, given a warm summer's day of course Retrace your steps to the cemetery, if preferred keeping to the left hand side of the strip of trees. The contour on your left follows the route of Quadrangle Alley.

Contalmaison Cemetery was near the junction of Pearl Alley and Quadrangle Support trench. It was here that Lieutenant Stanbury was last seen.

OTHER CEMETERIES & MEMORIALS

HEILLY STATION CEMETERY

The village was originally built around a magnificent chateau owned by members of the French aristocracy with Royal connections. It was destroyed in the French Revolution in 1847 and only a part of the south-east wing remained. Now that stands in ruins. Parts of the vast ramparts still remain and some remains of the outbuildings can still be found in the village.

XV Corps had their Headquarters here but exactly where is not known. Just outside the village over the railway line is Heilly Station Cemetery which actually stands within the communal boundary of Mericourt L´Abbé. It was the site of a casualty clearing station which was started in April 1916. It was exceptionally busy during those early days of July 1916 so much so that as the men died, so they were buried three to a grave in many cases, there being no time to dig all the graves. The ambulance trains plied their trade from the nearby railway line.

In the colonnades are engraved the cap badges of all the Regiments represented here, there being no space on the gravestones. Many of the wounded from the action described in this book were brought here. Just over the railway line going back towards the village turn left into an area signposted Étangs Fédéreux. Here will be found a beautiful recreation area in which it is possible to walk and picnic but patronised mainly by local fishermen who fish the waters of the beautiful lakes to be found there and possibly also utilised by the many troops who were billeted or bivouacked in the village.

MORLANCOURT BRITISH CEMETERY NUMBER ONE

This cemetery is situated amongst pleasant meadow land to the west of the village. It can only be approached on foot, a pleasant walk of some 500 metres through a small gate on the left that it is easy to miss, off the single track approach road. Among the graves are some of those wounded in the battles described and were brought back to Morlancourt and includes that of Lieutenant-Colonel O S Flower, commanding officer of the 13th Royal Welsh Fusiliers.

GORDON DUMP CEMETERY

It is a walk of about 200 metres to reach this cemetery which is situated on the Ovillers - Contalmaison road about one kilometre from Ovillers and signposted to the right.It contains the graves of some of the men from the regiments fighting in Pearl Alley and the Quadrangle. They include Captain J H Betts, MC of the Manchesters and Captain J A Benjamin of the 9th Duke of Wellingtons. Also in this cemetery is the grave of Second-Lieutenant D S Bell who won the Victoria Cross attacking a machine gun post at Horseshoe Trench near Contalmaison. In the plot immediately to the left of the entrance gate are some graves of men of the 8th South Staffordshire Regiment.

THE THIEPVAL MEMORIAL

The Thiepval Memorial commemorates those who fought in the Battle of the Somme and have no known grave. Stands high on the ridge and is a landmark which can be seen from many distant vantage points. It was designed by Sir Edwin Lutyens and was dedicated in July 1932 by the Prince of Wales. There are over 73,000 names on the memorial and many names of those killed in the battles described in this book are recorded here. Behind the memorial as you approach from the main entrance is a cemetery laid out with French graves on the left and British graves on the right which was created to symbolise the fraternity between the two nations. The registers are kept in bronze safes at either side of the steps leading up to the altar. In case of difficulty call at the work base at the left of the entrance and ask for Mr Paul Price, the Thiepval Area Supervisor or telephone the Commonwealth War Graves Commission Office at Beaurains 0321710324.

PRINCIPAL OFFICERS AND MEN INCLUDED IN THIS GUIDE

Throughout the book the names of some of the men involved in the action have been included. Where it has been possible to trace an outcome, these names have been listed below in chronological order as they appear in the book and in those cases where this has resulted in the existence of a grave or a name on a memorial, it is hoped that this will be helpful and interesting to the reader in making their visits.

Captain G S Dickinson, 7th Lincolnshire Regiment, killed in action 2.7.16 was buried at Peronne Road Cemetery, Maricourt.

Second Lieutenant W Turney, 8th South Staffordshire Regiment, was subsequently killed in action 10.7.16 and is commemorated on the Thiepval Memorial to the Missing of the Somme.

Lieutenant B L Kimber, 7th Lincolnshire Regiment, subsequently killed in action 10.7.16 is commemorated on the Thiepval Memorial to the Missing of the Somme.

Lieutenant T C Barrett, 7th Lincolnshire Regiment, died of wounds 4.7.16 was buried at Mericourt L´Abbé Communal Cemetery Extension.

Lieutenant P A H Thornilley, 21st Manchester Regiment, was subsequently promoted to Captain and won the Military Cross. He was killed in action on 11.1.17 and was buried in Beaumont-Hamel British Cemetery.

Lieutenant I W Usher, 2nd Royal Irish Regiment, killed in action 4.7.16 and was buried in Dantzig Alley British Cemetery.

Second Lieutenant F Kerr, 2nd Royal Irish Regiment, killed in action 4.7.16 is commemorated on the Thiepval Memorial to the Missing of the Somme.

Captain T L Crosse, 7th Border Regiment, killed in action 3.7.16 was buried at Dantzig Alley British Cemetery.

Second Lieutenant H H Crompton, 7th Border Regiment, killed in action 3.7.16 was buried at Dantzig Alley British Cemetery.

Brigadier-General R B Fell, commanding 51 Brigade was relieved by Brigadier-General G F Trotter on 6 July. According to Trotter, Brigadier-General Fell only knew of his relief when he (Trotter) arrived to take over.

Lieutenant J Dadd, 1st Royal Welsh Fusiliers, a friend of Siegfried Sassoon and Robert Graves was severely wounded. He also spent some time in a mental institution before recovering.

Captain P J G Ralph 2nd Royal Irish Regiment, was subsequently killed in action 6.8.17 and buried at Brandhoek Military Cemetery, Belgium.

Captain R W P Bell, 2nd Royal Irish Regiment, killed in action 5.7.16 is commemorated on the Thiepval Memorial to the Missing of the Somme.

Second Lieutenant G J D White, 2nd Royal Irish Regiment, killed in action 5.7.16 is commemorated on the Thiepval Memorial to the Missing of the Somme.

Second Lieutenant F Drummond, 9th Northumberland Fusiliers, killed in action 5.7.16 and buried in Gordon Dump Military Cemetery near La Boisselle.

Major J S Allen, 9th Northumberland Fusiliers, was awarded the Military Cross as a result of this action and was subsequently killed in action on 11.4.18 and is commemorated on the Ploegsteert Memorial, Belgium.

Company-Sergeant-Major F Green DCM, 9th Duke of Wellingtons

Regiment, killed in action 7.7.16 is commemorated on the Thiepval Memorial to the Missing of the Somme.

Captain A J Benjamin, 9th Duke of Wellingtons Regiment, killed in action 7.7.16 is buried in Gordon Dump Cemetery

Lieutenant L D Stanbury, 52 Brigade Machine Gun Corps, killed in action 7. 7. 16 is commemorated on the Thiepval Memorial to the Missing of the Somme.

Lieutenant L Holroyd, 7th East Yorkshire Regiment, subsequently wounded and died on 12. 9. 16 while awaiting embarkation to England and was buried at Etretat near Boulougne.

Lieutenant R P Albertanson, 6th Dorset Regiment, was awarded the Military Cross as a result of this action.

Second Lieutenant J K Michell, 52 Brigade Machine Gun Corps, was awarded the Military Cross for leading the search for Lieutenant Stanbury.

Private H Cocks, 52 Brigade Machine Gun Corps, was awarded the Distinguished Conduct Medal as a result of this action.

Major J R Angus, was later promoted Lieutenant-Colonel, transferred to the 11th South Wales Borderers and was drowned on 17th September 1917 and is buried in Erquinghem-Lys Churchyard Extension, France.

Captain J L Williams, 16th Welsh Regiment, died of wounds 12.7.16 and is buried at Corbie Communal Cemetery.

Company Sergeant Major R Thomas, 16th Welsh Regiment, killed in action 7.7.16 is commemorated on the Thiepval Memorial to the Missing of the Somme.

Lieutenant A Tregaskis, 16th Welsh Regiment, killed in action 7.7.16 is buried in Flat Iron Copse Cemetery.

Lieutenant L Tregaskis, 16th Welsh Regiment, killed in action 7.7.16 is buried in Flat Iron Copse Cemetery.

Private C Morgan, 16th Welsh Regiment, killed in action 7.7.16 is commemorated on the Thiepval Memorial to the Missing of the Somme.

Private H J Morgan, 16th Welsh Regiment, killed in action 7.7.16 is commemorated on the Thiepval Memorial to the Missing of the Somme.

Private A T Oliver, 16th Welsh Regiment, killed in action 7.7.16 is buried in Flat Iron Copse Cemetery

Private E Oliver, 16th Welsh Regiment, killed in action 10.7.16 is buried in Dantzig Alley British Cemetery

Lieutenant T Pryce-Hamer, 11th South Wales Borderers, killed in action 7.7.16 is commemorated on the Thiepval Memorial to the Missing of the Somme

Lieutenant-Colonel S J Wilkinson, commanding officer of the 10th South Wales Borderers, died of wounds 7.7.16 is commemorated on the Thiepval

Memorial to the Missing of the Somme

Sergeant E Taylor, 52 Brigade Machine Gun Corps, killed in action 6.7.16 is commemorated on the Thiepval Memorial to the Missing of the Somme.

Private E W Gibbs, 52 Brigade Machine Gun Corps, killed in action 6.7.16 is commemorated on the Thiepval Memorial to the Missing of the Somme.

Private W Gibson, Northumberland Fusiliers attached to 52 Brigade Machine Gun Corps, killed in action 6.7.16 is commemorated on the Thiepval Memorial to the Missing of the Somme.

Lieutenant-Colonel R J W Carden, 17th Lancers commanding the 16th Royal Welsh Fusiliers, killed in action 10.7.16 was buried at Carnoy Military Cemetery.

Major R H Mills, 14th Royal Welsh Fusiliers, killed in action 10.7.16 was buried in Dantzig Alley British Cemetery

Captain J Glynn Jones, 14th Royal Welsh Fusiliers was awarded the Military Cross for his work in evacuating the wounded.

Captain L P Godfrey, 14th Welsh Regiment died of wounds 23.8.17 and was buried at Mendinghem Military Cemetery, Proven, Belgium.

Lieutenant F J Hawkins, 14th Welsh Regiment was awarded the Military Cross as a result of this action.

Major G D'A Edwardes, 1st Dragoon Guards, commanding the 13th Welsh Regiment, killed in action 10.7.16 and was buried at Dantzig Alley British Military Cemetery.

Second Lieutenant H B Cowie, 10th Welsh Regiment, killed in action 10.7.16 and was buried at Dantzig Alley British Military Cemetery.

Second Lieutenant H H T Rees, 16th Royal Welsh Fusiliers, killed in action 10.7.16 is commemorated on the Thiepval Memorial to the Missing of the Somme.

Major L E Bond, 13th Welsh Regiment, killed in action 10.7.16 is commemorated on the Thiepval Memorial to the Missing of the Somme.

Second Lieutenant T P Purdie, 13th Welsh Regiment, killed in action 10.7.16 is commemorated on the Thiepval Memorial to the Missing of the Somme.

Second Lieutenant G D M Crossman, 13th Welsh Regiment, killed in action 10.7.16 is buried in Flat Iron Copse Cemetery.

Lieutenant-Colonel O S Flower, commanding the 13th Royal Welsh Fusiliers, died of wounds 12.7.16 was buried in Morlancourt British Cemetery No 1.

Major P Anthony, 15th Royal Welsh Fusiliers, killed in action 10.7.16 is commemorated on the Thiepval Memorial to the Missing of the Somme.

Lieutenant J Evans, 15th Welsh Regiment, was awarded the Military Cross as a result of this action.

Second Lieutenant W S A Clarke, 6th Dorset Regiment, killed in action 10.7.16 is commemorated on the Thiepval Memorial to the Missing of the Somme.

Lieutenant R B Cracroft, 7th East Yorkshire Regiment, killed in action 10.7.16 and is buried in Flat Iron Copse Cemetery.

Captain T Heathcock, 7th East Yorkshire Regiment, killed in action 10.7.16 is believed to have been buried in Flat Iron Copse Cemetery.

Second Lieutenant W H Cullen, 113th Brigade Machine Gun Company, killed in action 11.7.16 is commemorated on the Thiepval Memorial to the Missing of the Somme.

Second Lieutenant A Rosser, 14th Welsh Regiment, killed in action 10.7.16 is commemorated on the Thiepval Memorial to the Missing of the Somme.

Lieutenant D Yorke, 14th Welsh Regiment, was awarded the Distinguished Service Order as a result of this action.

Major D Hughes Onslow, 6th Dorset Regiment, killed in action 10.7.16 was buried in Meaulte Military Cemetery.

Private S Hicks, 6th Dorset Regiment, was awarded the Military Medal as a result of this action. He was killed in action 30.3.18. and is commemorated on the Arras Memorial to the Missing

Lance Corporal W Routliffe, 6th Dorset Regiment, was awarded the Military Medal as a result of this action.

Captain G O'Hanlon, 6th Dorset Regiment, was awarded the Military Cross for his part in this action.

Lieutenant G L Davidson, 6th Dorset Regiment, died of wounds 11.7.16 and was posthumously awarded the Military Cross. He was buried at Heilly Station Cemetery.

Captain L A P Harris, 16th Welsh Regiment, killed in action 11.7.16. is buried in Dantzig Alley Cemetery.

Captain E D Job, Artist's Rifles attached to 114th Brigade Machine Gun Corps, killed in action 11.7.16 is buried in Flat Iron Copse Cemetery.

HARRY FELLOWS' MEMORIAL

Harry Fellows was not a Welshman, nor was he even numbered among those from further afield from the Welsh borders who made up the numbers of the 38th Welsh Division. He was, though, always moved by the memory of what he experienced and in particular the task of burying the dead. In later years he returned to Mametz Wood and came to love the now peaceful valley and the rich and verdant countryside. The Wood itself restored and full of birdsong moved Harry to write one of his many poems.

Harry died not long after the Red Dragon was dedicated on 1 September 1987. He was present at the ceremony and spoke then of Mametz Wood as being 'no finer resting place' for the men he had buried. Through the efforts of his family and the generosity of the Comte de Thézy who owns the wood and who also gave the land on which the Red Dragon stands, Harry's ashes were interred in the wood as he had requested and a special memorial was erected. It stands where the central ride came out at the northern edge of the wood, close to Middle Alley and where Harry and Private Templeton held their lone vigil. It can be viewed by walking down the track leading into the wood off the Contalmaison-Longueval Road which lies east of the access road to Flat Iron Copse Cemetery. The memorial is on the right soon after the wood is entered.

Mametz Wood 1916 and 1984

Shattered trees and tortured earth
The acrid stench of decay
Of mangled bodies lying around
The battle not far away
This man made devastation
Does man have no regrets
Does he pause to ask the question
Will the birds sing again in Mametz?

This Welsh lad lying near my feet
With blood matted auburn hair
Was his father proud when he went to the war
Did his mother shed a tear
Did he leave a girl behind him
Awaiting the postman's knock
Oh! The sadness when they learn of his death
Dear God help them to bear the shock

That German boy, his bowels astrew
Fought for his Fatherland
That he fought to the last is obvious
A stick bomb is still in his hand
Did he hate us so much as we thought
Was our enmity so just
On his belt an insignia GOT MIT UNS
Did not the same God favour us
As 'far as the eye can see
Dead bodies cover the earth
The death of a generation
Condemned to die at birth
When comes the day of reckoning
Who will carry the can
For this awful condemnation
Of man's inhumanity to man
What a wondrous pleasant sight
Unfolds before my eyes
A panoply of magnificent trees
Stretching upwards to the skies
Did someone help Dame Nature
The sins of man to forget
Where once there was war now peace
reigns supreme
And the birds sing again in Mametz!

HARRY FELLOWS 1896 - 1987

INDEX

Robinson S Pte. 108
Rosser A Lt. 112, 171
Routliffe W LCpl. 74, 171
Rowley L A Lt Col. 70

Sassoon S 2 Lt. 23, 26, 37 - 40, 44, 74, 132, 165
Smith J Sgt. 51, 52, 71
Stanbury L D Lt. 49, 51, 52, 71, 72, 169

Taylor E Sgt. 49, 170,
Thorniley P A H Lt. 19, 20, 168
Thomas R C.S.M. 61, 65, 169
Tregaskis A Lt. 62, 63, 167
Tregaskis L Lt. 62, 63, 167
Turney W Lt. 16, 168

Usher I W Lt. 26, 168

Walmsley Alan 147
Watts H E Major General 35, 77, 78, 84, 105, 106, 113, 119, 134
Wilkinson S J Lt Col. 64, 169
Williams J L Captain 61, 65, 169

Yorke D Lt. 112, 171

PLACE NAMES

Acid Drop Copse 52, 86, 88 - 90, 107, 109
Albert 145, 147
Bolton 47
Botton Wood 19, 20, 22, 33, 37, 52, 56
Cardiff 47
Caterpillar Wood 59, 60, 62, 65, 66, 93, 102
Contalmaison 36, 50, 51, 53, 68, 73, 79, 83, 87, 115
Death Valley 128, 129, 130
Flat Iron Copse 61, 102, 117
Fricourt 16, 33, 46, 52, 54, 150
Fricourt Chateau 33, 49, 83, 161,162
Fricourt Wood 19, 21
Grovetown 44, 75, 84
Hammerhead 50, 61, 66, 68, 101, 102,

117, 121
Heilly 15, 44, 66, 75, 76, 77, 84, 113, 116, 130, 166
Mametz Wood 14, 18, 21, 23, 24, 37, 43, 45, 49, 55, 58, 68, 79, 91 - 113, 150
Marlborough Copse 43, 93, 102
Meaulte 15, 33, 54
Pommiers Redoubt 60, 64, 67, 101
Quadrangle Wood 21, 22,
Queen's Nullah 65 - 67, 96. 120
Railway Copse 46
Sabot Copse 61
Shelter Wood 21
Swansea 47
Treux 62
Verdun 12
Walsall 47

TRENCHES

Bottom Alley 19, 20, 42
Cliff Trench 18, 22, 68
Crucifix Trench 21
Danzig Alley 60, 96
Hedge Line Trench 34, 36, 46
Lozenge Trench 16, 161
Middle Alley 112, 113, 122
Montauban Alley 43, 59, 60
Pearl Alley 36, 49, 51, 53, 73, 79, 86
Quadrangle Alley 42, 50, 55 - 58, 69, 73, 74, 79 - 81, 109, 115, 116
Quadrangle Support 42, 43, 49, 50, 51, 53, 55 - 58, 68, 69, 73, 74, 78 - 81, 85 - 90, 114 -116
Quadrangle Trench 21, 22, 24, 34 - 36, 27, 42, 44 - 46, 50 - 53, 74, 79, 81
Railway Alley 16, 19, 21
Shelter Alley 36, 44, 50
Shelter Wood 19, 21, 49
Strip Trench 25 - 31, 41, 50, 68, 70, 75, 91, 92, 96, 158
White Trench 18, 22, 91
Wood Trench 35 - 41, 50, 58, 69, 81, 92, 99, 158
Wood Support Trench 99, 105, 107, 109, 114 - 116, 158